THE ZELIANGRONG NAGAS
(*A Study of Tribal Christianity*)

JWP PUBLICATIONS

Status of Rural Women in India	75.00
Status of Nurses in India	60.00
Status of Women in the Quran (Urdu)	5.00
Status of Single Women in India	125.00
Status of Banjara Women in India	125.00
Trafficking in Wemen and Children in India	125.00
Women in Organised Movements	45.00
Child Labour in Bangalore City	30.00
Customary Laws and Women in Manipur	150.00
A Socio-Economic Survey of Slum Dwellers in Caluutta	15.00
Women's Decade (An Assessment)	30.00
The Problem of Dowry in Bangalore City	5.00
Indian Women in Media	12.00
Women and Law	5.00
Prostitution with Religious Sanction (Devadasi/Jogini)	20.00
Changes in Christian Personal Laws	3.50
Christian Marriage and the Customary Practices in Manipur	15.00
The Shahbano Controversy	125.00
Women in CNI Diocese of Delhi	5.00
Wake Up and Live	5.00
Female Sexuality in Hinduism	10.00
Women's Participation in Political Parties in U.P. (Hindi)	250.00
Women in the Freedom Struggle (Hindi)	25.00
Authority of the Religions and the Status of Women	50.00
Pavement Dwellers of Calcutta	15.00
Cultural Chotanagpur : Unity in Diversity	175.00
The Legalization of Prositution	60.00
The Zeliangrong Nagas : A Study of Tribal Christianity.	200.00

THE ZELIANGRONG NAGAS
(A STUDY OF TRIBAL CHRISTIANITY)

REV. RAMKHUN PAMEI

Under the Auspices of
WILLIAM CAREY STUDY AND
RESEARCH CENTRE

UPPAL PUBLISHING HOUSE
NEW DELHI—110002 (INDIA)

UPPAL PUBLISHING HOUSE
3, Ansari Road, Daryaganj, New Delhi-110002
Phones : *Off.* 3273756, 3286571 *Res.* 2242884

First Published 1996
ISBN 81-85565-68-6

Printed in India

Published by B.S. Uppal for Uppal Publishing House
3, Ansari Road, Daryaganj, New Delhi - 110002
and Printed at Sainion Printary, Delhi - 110032.

CHALLENGE OF DEDICATED OF THIS BOOK

'AM I A SOLDIER OF THE CROSS ?'

In 1864 Edward Payson Scott, a missionary, entered Naga Hills where even the British invaders dreaded to go. Scott armed only with a Bible and a violin set off for the hills. As he climed up the rugged hills, he saw ahead of him 'twelve naked Naga warriors with spears raised to strike' and quickly he put his violin to chin and began to play the hymn "Am I a soldier of the cross" The warriors were entranced and befriended. They conveyed, "You may come and stay among us as long as you wish if you bring that violin with you." Scott having made the contract told them of the one true God who loved all his creatures. "Thus the mountain fastness of the dreaded Nagas was broken by the sweet strains of a violin" and the we hear praises to day.

Dadicated to my beloved Tamenglong Village Baptist Church for God's glory and the extension of His Kingdom; Halleluiyah !

Tharon Naga Village
Imphal

March 26, 1996

Foreword

Anyone who attempts to write about the history of Christianity in North-East India is faced by a number of formidable obstacles. The repidly growing Christian community in that region is distributed among at least eighty different tribal groups. Each of these groups has its own language, culture and history. Some have lived in their present homes for thousands of years, others are still in the process of migration across the international boundary. Some have preserved their tribal traditions in the form of folk stories, songs, dances and other art forms have almost totally lost knowledge of their cultures prior to the advent of the modern period.

The modern period, which was inroduced in the hill areas through their gradual annexation by the British during the nineteenth century, has also brought different reactions among the different tribes among which Christians are found. Some were able to accommodate themselves to the new order after only minimal resistance, others continued to resist the irreversible tides of modernization for a longer period. Some lived in areas that contituted single administrative units under the British, others found their traditional homelands divided among several administrative units, thus making the development of institutions of tribal identity more difficult.

No one knows better than I how this complex context complicates the work of historical study for the region as a whole. Until very recently all the scholarly studies of

Christianity in the region were done by outsiders like myself. Even for persons who belong to North-East India the problem of linguistic diverstiy makes it very difficult to gain access to the sources. No historian, whether an outsider or a person from the region itself, knows more than a few of those eighty languages in which some of the most important sources have been written. Most of us are confined to sources written in the English language. This means that we mainly rely on mission and government sources, rather than materials that reflect the understandings of the people who make up the membership of the churches concerned.

The linguistic problem is going to remain. Even the most accomplished linguist is not going to be able to master more than a fraction of the indigenous sources. For some time to come, the academic link-language must be English. For the progress of the historical study of Christianity in the region based upon indigenous sources there will have to be another link, what might be called the link-historian. The link-historian is a person trained in historical method who knows both English and an indigenous language, usings her or his mother tongue. These historians use the indigenous language sources but write in English so that the fruits of their research are made available to the larger community of scholars.

Ramkhun Pamei provides such a link it this study. While I myself have studied the history of Christianity among the Zeliangrong Nagas, those studies have always been limited and superficial because I did not know the languages necessary to study those sources which contain the perspective to the people concerned. Ramkhun has, through this book, added one more title to a still small but nevertheless growing list of link-histories. As these micro-studies multiply, macro-studies of the history of Christianity in the region as a whole will become much more reliable.

In many ways the Zeliangrong Christians have a unique history. They were among those who were scattered across administrative borders by the British, a situation that has been perpetuated in independent India, and therefore for a long time did not develop the tribal cohesiveness that those tribes did who lived within single administrative districts. The problem of the development of tribal identity was also made difficult by the fact that the Zeliangrong are a composite of three distinct but closely related tribes, the Zeme, Liangmei and Rongmei. Another factor that delayed the development of a tribal identity was the existence of two major religious movements among them in the modern period. For a half century these two movements worked against each other. One was Christianity, the other was the nativistic movement led by Jaduanang and carried on by Rani Gaidinliu. Though today many Zeliangrong Christians, including Ramkhun, look upon this movement as an expression of Zeliangrong sub-natioual identity in rebellion against the British, historically it represented a religious movement directly opposed to the advancement of Christianity among the tribe. One of the important contributions of this book is in showing how a religious movement based upon a religious world-view strongly anti-Christian in character has been reinterpreted and transformed into a movement promoting a unitary identity for the entire tribe, including Christians.

My point is not to pass judgment on the historical significance of the Zeliangrong Rebellion of the 1930s, but simply to point out the unique elements in the history of Christianity among one tribe in the North-East. Christianity among the Zeliangrong developed within a wholly unique historical context. The contribution the Ramkhun has made to the study of both the context and the growth of the Christian movement within it is of great value. All historians of Christianity owe him much for the hard work that he has done in researching for and writing this book over a period of yerrs.

I count it a privilege to have been his teacher many years ago, and fellow worker within the family of the Council of Baptist Churches in North-East India ever since.

Bangalore **FREDERICK S. DOWNS**

Preface

The younger generation, when they encounter the situation of life in changing society, there is likelihood of their lossing the meaning and relevance of faith. It will be improper to pass judgement and to plan for the present situation intelligently without the knowledge of the past history. So the Zeliangrong Church needs to be informed of its past history, religion, social, political and economic life. Their traditions hand customs need to be preserved. Their occupation, land and environment in which they have been brought up need to be studied. And also how the Gospel was communicated so that the Church may knew where she was, when she is and where she is going.

The history of the communication of the Gospel as such has not been written so far. Therefore, the author feels that writing such history will help in planning its work at present and for future. Inspite of scarcity of materials the author has endeavoured to glimpes into the history and spreading the Gospel among the Zeliangrong Nagas in North-East India.

The Zeliangrong has no other literature of their own except some books written by British writers. I have made use of them much to portray the historical background of the people. As for the mission work of the Church, however, most of them are authentic materials gathered from the older Church people.

The last two chapters deal with the present secular world situation with which the Church is confrented. As civilization advances among the people it is worthwhile to reexamine the position of the Church. This is necessary because the Church is for the world and its ministry is for the world in which it exists.

I am indebted to several people for help in writing this book. I acknowledge with gratitude the help I have received from my Zeliangrong Baptist Association Workers particularly Rev. M.P. Namthiurei, Field Secretary, Rev. Z.G. Dinthuiyang, Superintendent Pastor, Mr. P. Meingan, Field Director, the Elders of my own Local Baptist Church Tamenglong Village from which I have received oral information as well as writen materials which enabled me to write this book. A special word of appreciation is due to K. Gangmumei, of Manipur University who has given valuable advice and help in collecting materials for the first sections. I wish to extend my hearty thanks to the Librarian of the Secretariat Office of the State of Manipur and the Central Library of Imphal for allowing me to use their Libraries. I had also interviewed and had discussed with Mr. Heutui, Executive Secretary of ZNBA, Mr. Namrigwang Executive Secretary of LNBA, Nagaland who supplied some basic materials and also Rev. H. Visor who was the Executive Secretary of the Zeliangrong Baptist Church Council, Nagaland and at present the General Secretary of the Council of the Naga Baptist Churches who supplied materials on Zeliangrong Baptist history in Nagaland. My special gratitude and thanks go to also Mr. Dichamand Pamei who helped me by supplying material on Zeliangrong Festival—Malanmei and Mr. D. Athuibou Ex-MLA for narrating me to the origin of Zeliangrong people.

I wish to extend my hearty thanks to Rev. Lynn Buzzard Asst. Professor of Ministry and Director of Field Education of the Northern Baptist Theological Seminary, Chicago, U.S.A. who has given valuable advice and suggestions. My thanks are also due to Mrs. Karen Bannen, English teacher of the same Seminary, for the initial conection of Language. I am also very indebted and grateful to Miss. Ashin Panmei, Principal of the Mount Zion English School for minute correction of the English, re-editing and typing and re-reading the whole manuscript. Special gratitude of my heart extend to Dr. F.S. Downs the Professor in U.T.C. Bangalore and my former teacher at ETC Jorhat, Assam for the valuable suggestions, advice and for correcting the writing in this book. To many other friends whose names are not mentioned here, I am indebted greatly for their encouragement in bringing out this book.

REV. RAMKHUN PAMEI

Contents

Chapters		Pages
	Foreword	*vii*
	Preface	*xi*
I.	INTRODUCTION	1
	1. Background History of the Zeliangrong Social Landscape—The Hevering Past—2. Background History of Nagaland – Origin of Nagaland as a State Tribes and Clans—Migration 3. Background History of Manipur—The Land and Zeliangrong Naga—The People and their Origin—Zeliangrong Naga and Life—Music and Dance—Economic Life -- Social Life—Morung—Malunmei—Religious Idea—Life after Death—Zeliangrong Rebellion.	
II.	THE FIRST COMMUNICATION OF THE GOSPEL AMONG THE ZELIANGRONG	42
	Prediction of the Coming of Christianity—Early Missionaries—The First Convert of Rongmeis Among the Zeliangrong Nagas, Manipur—The First Baptist Church in the Zeliangrong Area—Persecution—Beginning of Christsanity Among the Zeliangrong Naga in Nagaland and Assam—The Lingmei Baptist Association—Rougmei Baptist Association—The Zeliangrong Nagas in Assam—Reinforcement of Mission Work— Revival—Outcome of Revival—Conviction of Sin—Judgement –Amazing Result—Travailing in Prayer—Eagerness in Evangelism—The Living Standard—Social Economic and Political Awareness—Kangpokpi Mission Compound.	

Chapters *Pages*

III. EDUCATION IN THE EARLY MISSION 83

Christion Schools—The Second World War and its Effect—Organization of the Church for the Mission—Later Missionaries.

IV. DEVELOPMENT OF THE PROPAGATION OF THE GOSPEL 92

Establishment of Christian Centre—Youth Fellowship—Women Society—Division of Circles in the Association—Self Support and Self Propagation—Literature—Bible Translation Works.

V. THE CONTEMPORARY SITUATION 108

Formation of the Zeliangrong Union—Demand for a Zeliangrong Homeland—Some of the Characteristic of Zeliangrong Nagas—The Impact of Modern Secular Trends on the Church—The Effect of Education on Christian Youth—The Church in Relation to its Environment.

VI. EVALUATION OF SOME ASPECTS OF THE GOSPEL IN THE CHURCH 122

Renewal of the Church for its Mission—Renewal of the Corporate Spiritual Life—Involvement in the World—Indigenisation—Song and Dance—Faith—Architecture—The Zeliangrong Church in the Future.

VII. BIOGRAPHIES NAMRIJINANG KAMEI MAIPAK 133

Pakho Sithlou—Maisi Newmei—A. Pariwangbou.

BIBLIOGRAPHY 145

INDEX 150

CHAPTER I

Introduction

1. Background History of the Zeliangrongs

The Zeliangrong country which covers a compact and contiguous area includes, even during the Colonial days, the North-West Sub-division of Manipur State (now Tamenglong District, Sadar Hills, Mao west, Loktak Project area and Jiribam), Halflong circles of North Cachar Hills and Sub-division of Cachar District of Assam (now Peren Sub-division of Nagaland). Historically, the Zeliangrong territory covered the whole mountain tract from the Dhaneswa river in the North to the confluence of Chin hills of Burma in the South, from the Bhuvan hills, eastern Cacher plains of Barak valley and Jaintia hills of eastern Meghalaya in the West, to the Koubru Laimaton range overlooking the beautiful Imphal valley, the Mao Maram hills in the East. The southern boundary, since the middle of the nineteenth century according to British ethnographers, was at the latitude 24.70 degree North running across Northern Churachandpur District of Manipur, from Bhuvan hills. According to the English ethnographers like McCulloch, Brown and Hodson the southern ethnic boundary of the Zeliangrong country was one day's journey to the South of the Manipur Cachar Bridle Path, popularly known as the Rongjei Maril in Manipur (the bamboo tube line so called because of the narrow and precipitous topography of the path). The Bridle path was improved by the British engineers using tribal labour in 1835-39, and further expanded into a fine weather motorable road, a century later, during the Second World War by Col. Chapman's pioneers. This little bridle path was the silent witness to the changing fortunes of the Manipuri kings and rulers, bloody encounters during the Burmese invasions in the eighteenth and nineteenth centuries, the passage of the colonial military officers whose writings, specially of R.B. Pemberton, R. Brown and James Johnstone have immortalised this path. It was one of the four important trade routes connecting Manipur valley with the rest of India. Thousands of people, soldiers, traders, conquerors, kings and rulers had passed through this path from Imphal, the capital town of Manipur State.[1]"

The Zeliangrong habitat covering an area of more than ten thousand sq kms is situated over the northern, southern and western branches of the great Barail range of the eastern Himalayan system. These stiff mountains, deep gorges and the river valley provide shelter, sustenance and protection to the ancestors of the Zeliangrong people who had moved into the land more than 5,000 years ago. The important hill ranges and peaks of the region which are interwoven with myths and traditions of the dwellers are the Paona and Peren ranges in the Northern spur of Mt. Zapfu in Nagaland, the Halflong slopes in the western spur of the great Barail in Assam, the Makui Longdi range running southward from Mt. Tenipu in Mao area of northern Manipur, connecting with the Koubru Laimaton range, being bisected by the upper reaches of the Barak river. The highest peak being Mt. Koubru. the landing place of God, between Koubru-Laimaton range and the Cachar plains, there are saveral ranges of varying sizes and heights of the traditional nine ranges between Manipur and Cachar starting from Assam side,

1. R. Brown, A Statiscal account of Manipur, Calcutta, 1874 (Reprint, 1975 Delhi), p. 15.

one has to climb up the low lying Taosem or Vengai range and Nungjaband, then crossing the Makru river, climb up the Oinamlong or Kala Naga range (3600 ft.) then make a descent to the Barak river and climb up to Kambiton, then to Nungba range (3450 ft.), then march to Mongjoron Khulel and make another descent to the Irang and climb up to Khoupum range, west of Khoupum valley. Starting from this valley, one has to climb up the Napsinmei or Phourungba range (4700 ft.) than climb down to Leimatak and descend to the Laimaton-Ngariyal peak (5600ft) and down to Bishnupur in the south Manipur valley. Other peaks associated with legends and traditions of the Zeliangrong people are the Paona, Gadaibut. Pankibut, Khoupum, Kasuakbut, Hangrum Kacha Khou in Northern Tamenglong.

The rivers are the great Barak and the Irang. The Barak known as Ahu. the Irang, known as Alang are so much intermingled with the folklora and worldview of the Zeliangrong people that poets and singers refer to the Barak as mother and the Irang as the father. Even the Milky Way in the sky is described as the heavenly Ahu and Alang (Barak and Irang). The Barak starting from Liyai in northern Mao, traverses the whole Zeliangrong country down to Tipaimikh, then running up to Jirimuk and then to Cachar where it turns into a demon of destruction and a creator of fertility of soil. The Irang, starting from the upper portion of the Koubru range, falls into the Barak in Churachandpur District; the Zuko which runs parallel with the Barak and Jiri falls into the Barak; the Makru flowing down from the Zepfu peak flows into the Barak. Other rivers like the Ijei and the Laimatak (Apin) flow into the Irang. The river basins of the Ijei and the Laimatak are very fertile areas; the Makru and Barak basins covering the whole taosem sub-division of Tamenglong district are the most inaccessible region.

Mention may be made of the beautiful Barak waterfalls (four stepfalls though it is also known as the seven step falls) between Sempang and Makoi villages and the four fresh water lakes on the west bank of Barak, a few kms. from the waterfalls, known as the Zeiled lakes. There are several natural caves, near Tharon village, a water-formed sandstone cave, and the Gave in the Bhuvan hills, the holy place of pilgrimage, discovered by Jadonagang and Gaidinliu. The Zeliangrong region is rich in natural resources, the forest and water from her big rivers, the valleys are the Khoupum valley, 30 sq. miles in size and the Zaluke valley.

Social Landscape

In the ethnic landscape of the north-east India, the Zeliangrong people are a unique example of the evolution of a common identity of a group of cognate tribes who were, though of common origin, seqarated by a hostile geography and history, followed by social non-communication and lack of common organisation. But now the same people have been united by the bonds of common origin, common kinship and common cultural heritage, reinforced by common experiences of suffering at the hands of the alien invaders. Zeliangrong is the acronym of the cognate tribes namely, Zame. Liangmei and Rongmei including Puimei (Ze + Liang + Rong) which was coined on Feb 15, 1947 to give a common name to the said group. Due to historical reasons, the Meiteis of Manipur and following them the British had given external names to them: Kacha Nagas meaning the Zeme and the Liangmei, Kabui meaning Rongmei and Puimei.

Ethnically and linguistically, the Zeliangrongs belong to the Tibeto-Burman group of southern Mongolia. G.A Grieson has grouped the Zeliangrong languages with the Naga-Bodo linguistic sub-family. The official names for the Zeliangrong tribes are different from state to state. In Manipur they are known as Kabui and Kacha Nagas ; in Nagaland, Zeliang is the official name, whereas in Assam separate names like Zeme and Rongmei are used. The people themselves very much desire to be called Zeliangrong as the common ethnic name and Zeme, Liangmei, Rongmei and Puipei are to be the dialectical names, The Zemes are found in Nagaland, Assam and North-West. Manipur; the Liangmeis are more or less confined to Manipur's Tamei, Tamenglong and the Sadar Hills sub-division with few villages in Nagaland; whereas the Rongmeis are the most dispersed group, as they are found in western Manipur, Imphal plains, Cacher plain and in Nagaland. The Puimeis are found only in nine villages of Manipur. During the last two decades or so, there have been lots of migrations and intermingling through marriages among them in the three states. In social organisation, religious and economic activities and organisations, the Zeliangrongs have vrey strong common features. The seemingly different dialecte spoken by them have linguistic affinity. Thus, Zeliangrong is a clear case of one ethno-cultural entity speaking dialects of common origin. The Zeliangrongs have great culural and linguistic affinities with the Marama and the Thangalas.

The Zeliangrong society is a patrilincal society with two moeties or major clans, namely, Pamet and Newmei which are further sub-divided into many exogamous clans and sub-clans. These two major clans are found in all the three major cognate tribes which are subdivided into different clans with different names. The clans have totems. For example, the Pamei is found in the four cognate groups. Among the Rongmeis, Pamei is divided into clans like Kamei, Phaomei, Singongmei, Kamson, Malangmei and the Pamei. They have one single totem, the wild green pigeon (Ahuina) which is the tabooed food for all the clans and the sub-clans of the Pamei mostly. However, Malangmei clan has the black monkey (Pang) as their totem. The Newmei is also found among the four cognate groups; they are sub-divided into Gonmei, Panmei, Riamei, Daimei, Abonmei, Dangmei, Thaimei, Rongmei, Gonthangmei etc. There are sub-clans also based on lineage or ancestry. Kinship, therefore, is the strongest base of Zeliangrong ethinc identity.

The Hovering Past

The Zeliangrong people have a strong sense of the their past. But their sense of the past is a mixture of myths, legends and traditions preserved in their ritual hymns, their songs and oral traditions. History to them is the oral tradition handed down through generations. They believe that the ancestors came out of a mythical cave called taobei perhaps a non existent place. They also believe that they sometime lived along with other Naga tribes at Makhel, now a Mao Noga village in North Manipur which was a point of dispersal in the story of migration. Of many Naga tribes like the Maos, the Tangkhuls, the Semas, the Angamis and the Chakhesamgs, it appears that the ancestors of the Zeliangrongs were in contact with the Dimasa Cacharis as evident from some folk songs. From Makhel, they came to a deep gorge called Ramtiag Kabin where they took shelter for sometime. Emerging from Ramting Kabin they came to settle down at a place which came to be known as Makui Longdi near the present Oklong village in Mao west. Here they led a settled life based on shifting agriculture. The village became very populous and number of houses according to tradition reached the incredible number of seven thousand seven hundred and seventy seven. Perhaps due to the non-availability of enough land for cultivation, internal differences among the ruling clans or failure of maintaining their religious life, different batches migrated from Makui Longdi. From the two relics of small stones found at Makui Longdi named Pamei and Newmei stones, it can be presumed that the people had developed into two major clans, the Mewmei clan and the Pamei clan. Traditions says that the sone of the chief of Makui Longdi went to Koubru mountain for settlement. Kaubru is called Regwang Phaipa, the landing place of God. A group of migrants went to the Northern and Western slopes of the Great Barail range in search of flat lands. They cams to be known as Zemo peolpe or the dwellers of the plain and hot land. Another group went towards the south which was an unoccupied barren land of the southern direction and inhabitants of the Maruong (west land) region came to be known as Maruongmei which was corrupted into Rongmei. Those who stayed back at Makui Longdi and in the nearby areas came to be known as Liangmei, the northerners. The southward migration of the people continued up to the confines of Chin hills of Burma and Mizoram covering the present Churachandpur District. Even today, there are large number of stone megaliths in the deserted or semi-deserted villages which were relics of the Zeliangrong habitation. The southern Zeliangrongs had to face the brunt of the old Kuki migration from Burma into Manipur. The migration came in batches of small groups in an extended period. Thus came the Koms, the Koirengs the Chirus, the Hmare and the Kourangs who were known to the Zeliangrongs as Koumei. The Zeliangrongs were further pushed up to the point which has been located at the latitude, by the British ethnographers at 24.70° north of the Equator. There are innumerable traditions of heroic fights between the Zeliangrong folk and culture heros against the Koumei intruders. The Zeliangrongs of the Barail range came into conflict with the Dimasa-Kachoris with their capital at Dimapur in Nagaland and later on at Maibong in north Cacher hills and further to Khaspur in Cavhar plains. The Kacharis and their rulers tried to established hegemony over the Zeliangrong people. There are historical anecdotes of fight between the Zeme hero Jamlennang with the Kacharis who ultimately killed him by a deceptive stratagem. The heroic fight, the courage and bravery of Jamlennang are preserved in popular tradititonal songs. In another tradition, the Kachari king forcibly took away Rengaonei, the beautiful wife of Nakam whose songs of mental agony and disappointment are sung even today.

The Meiteis' connection with the Zeliangrongs is quite ancient. The Meitei chronicles and historical text of Manipur refer to the relation between the two peoples. As stated above, the Tamenglong hills with its steep slopes and dense forests provided shelter to the fleeing Meitee princes during their rebellions and invasions from Burma. The Zeliangrong relations with the kings of Moirang in Southern Manipur valley are found in the Khamba-Thoibi epic of Moirang and in their folklores. There were repeated military conflicts between the Meitei rulers and the Zeliangrong villages of the Koubru-Laimaton range and the Ijei and Laimaton basins. The Zeliangrong village chief helped the king Gariba Niwaz of Manipur during his Burmese wars in the first half of the eighteenth century. His grandson king Bhagyachandra also took shelter under the Zeliangrongs during his liberation struggle against the Burmese. Even now there are relice connected with his sojourn in the Tamenglong hills. During the Burmese occupation of Manipur (1819-1826) which coincided with the 1st Anglo-Burmese war, the Zeliangrong people resisted the Burmese of invaders and helped the Manipupri princes. From the contemporary account, it is clear that the Zeliangrong people of western Manipur were independent of any alien rule during this period. We have, in this respect, the authority of R.B. Pemberton, a British officer who helped Gambhir Singh in the re-conquest of Manipur from the Burmese. It was Rajah Gambhir Singh of Manipur who first introduced administrative authority over the southern portions of the Zeliangrog country along the three trade routes: the Akhui route the old Cachar Load and Khongzai Road route. Cheitharel Kumbaba records the military expedition of Gambhir Singh to this region. One is tempted to quote Pemberton to have a view of the contemporary situation.

> "The whole track comprised between the Khongzai on the south and that of Aque on the north is occupied by Kupooees (Rongmei) tribe of Naga who are tributary to Manipur. Until the authority of Gambhir Singh had been firmly established over them they were engaged in constant warfare; travellers dared not venture to pass through the country except in large bodies, even then, were compelled to pay largely at every place for permission to continue their journey. Now, however, they

have been so effectively subjugated that dak man locally traverses the whole country with perfect safety and no single instance that I am aware of, has occurred in the large last eight years of their being attacked, stopped or plundered."[2]

The British started penetrating into northern Zeliangrong country since 1832 in connivance with Manipur. E.R. Grange, 'The father of Assam Rifle,' led the first expedition to the Zeme country. In 1865 the British formed the Naga Hill District with the Head Quarters at Asalu, a Zeliangrong village in Halfiong. The Manipur sector of the Zeliangrong areas was brought under the British rule with their conquest of Manipur in 1871. The Zeliangrong people opposed the imposition of house tax on them. Military expeditions were sent out to punish the Zeliangrong villāges of North-west Manipur under the command of Crawford, Assistant Political Agent of Manipur. During the Kuki rebellion (1917-1919) Zeliangrong villages of Manipur suffered most due to the British failure of providing protection to them, thus shaking the confidence of the people in the British rule. After the Kuki rebellion the North-West subdivision was with Tamenglong as the Head Quarter. The regular British administration was introduced in the Zeliangrong country. Earlier in Assam, regular British administration was established in Halflong area and Barema area of Naga Hills. Against this colonial backdrop, Jadonang emerged as a challenge to the British imperialism, opening a new chapter of resurgence in the Zeliangrong history.

2. Background History In Nagaland

Nagaland is the easternmost of the present twenty five states of the Indian Union. The State is triangular in shape having the vertex in the North and base in the South, and lies from

2 R.B. Pemberton, Report on North Eastern Frontier of British India, Reprint, 1966, Gauhati. pp. 54-55.

North-East to South-West. It is bounded by Assam all alongi ts west from North to South; Manipur in the South, Burma in the West and Arunachal Pradesh on the northern side of the eastern border. The total area of the State according to 1971 census is 16,527 sq. km. It is the third smallest in size among all the states of the Indian Union.

The State was created on 1st December 1963 as the 16th state of the Indian Union and is inhabited by 7,74,930 people according to 1981 census. Out of the total population, the scheduled tribes are 4,57,602 which includes Kukis, Kacharis and others who are not Nagas. So from population point of view the State may be called a tribal state and Christian by religion and it is the first of its kind in India.

The District of Naga Hills was opened in 1866 with its Head Quarter at Samaguting in the west on the foothills, some 15 km from Dimapur. Later, the District Head Quarter was shifted to Wokha in the hearts of the Hills in 1876. Two years later it was shifted to Kohima in 1878. More and more areas came under the administration. The present Tuensang and Mon District came under administration in 1948. In 1957 the Tuensang Frontier Division of North East Frontier Agency (Now Arunachal Pradesh) was separated from it and joined with Naga Hills to form Naga Hills Tuensang Area or NHTA. In short. In 1961 the NHTA became a de-facto State under the name Nagaland with de-fecto legislature and Ministry. In 1963 it was made a de-jure State. It was the time when the Naga people Convention decided for the recognition and listing the names of Tribal Naga groups, they missed out the name Rongmei which is one of the original cribes in Nagaland. The Rongmeis from time immemorial before the creation of the Nagaland State had been settling in Dimpur and Kohima as well. Leaving out the Rongmei, they listed Zeliang with the collection of Zeme and Liangmei. Now the Zeliangrong people Convention and the Rongmei Tribe are appealing for their rightful claim to the Government of Nagland for recognition and inclusion among the original Nagas in the Nagaland State.

Origin of Nagaland as State

During the British rule the Nagas did not grumble about the administration; they were independent by themselves. Due to more aggressive and frequent inter village feuds and head-huntings giving troubles even to the nearby Assam valley the extension of British administration was felt to bring into Naga Hills peace and tranquility among the Nagas. Thus, gradually, the administration extended all over the Naga Hills. But still then the Nagas were not united. Only in the later part of the British rule of seventy years (1876-1947) the different Nagas tribes felt that they were Nagas and one family. It is because of the teaching of the Gospe l of Jesus Christ which influenced such thinking.

When the Simon Commission visited Kohima in 1927 the Nagas Leaders pleaded that they should be left alone when the British left. It was from that time the thought came that it is the land of the Nagas. By the middle of this century the thought grounded and people started writing Nagaland instead of Naga Hills. Officially the term came into being in 1961 when the de-facto State of Nagaland was formed. That time it used to be written as Naga Land. Later it settled down as Nagaland, sometime after the State of Nagaland was formally inaugurated on 1st December 1963 by Dr. Radha Krishnan, the President of India.

Tribes and Clans

Originally Nagas were not known by the names of the tribes as they are known now, but by the name of a group of villages to some extent in some communities. Formally Phoms were included in the Konyak Tribe but now they are separated. In 1948, three tribes—Chakruma, Khezhama and Sangtam—together formed into one tribe called Chakhesang. This name was formed by taking Cha of Chakruma. Khe of Khesnama and Sang of Sangtam. Some small tribes such as Makwre, Chirr, Tikher etc. claim to be separate tribes now but then the nearby bigger tribes claim them to be an off shoot of theirs. As such the Zeliangrong Tibe Tribe is an amalgamation of Zemei, Liangmei and Rongmei. The Zeliangrongs are more akin to each other a due to their blood relationship of the same family in three dialective groups of Zemei, Liangmei and Rongmei.

According to the 1971 census there are 16 Naga tribes and four non Naga tribes inhabiting Nagaland. They are all scheduled tribes. They are Ao, Konyak, Sema, Chakhesang Angami, Lotha, Sangtam, Phom, change, Khaimengan, Yimchunger, Zeliengrong, Rengma, Tikhir, Mokware and Chirr. Non Naga tribes are Kuki, Kochari, Garo and Karbi.

Of the Naga tribes many Konyaks are living in Burma and many Rangmas are in Assam. Many Zeliangrongs are living in Assam, Manipur as well. It may be noted that Acs and Loths live in the west of the State. Kacharis, Garos and Karbis live in the west and south-west. The Zeliangrongs and Kukis live in the south-west. Angamis live in the south and south-west. Chakhesangs live in the south-east. Semas live in the centre of the State. Konyaks and Phoms live in the north and north-east. Rengmas live in the mid-south. Chang, Sangtam, Yimchunger, Khaimungan, Kokware, Chirr and Tikre live in the eastern side of the State which borders Burma.

Before the British took over and controlled Nagaland under their administration, Negaland covers the whole Tangkhul Naga areas now east of Manipur (Ukhrul District) and the whole Zeliangrong Nagas area now Tamenglong District, North Cachar Hills, west of Manipur, and also Mao Maram areas, now Senapati district in the north of Manipur. B.B. Ghosh said, "At the beginning in 1835 Manipur was invited to control

Ghosh; B.B. : History of Nagaland; S. Chand & Company Ltd. Ram Nagar, New Delhi. Published in 1982 pp. 145-46.

Naga Hills. Though the invitation was withdrawn later, some portion of southern Naga Hills now forming Mao and Tameng long sub-divisiod went to Manipur State."

Migration

The approximate time for migration of the Naga people to Naga Hills is given sometime in 1100 A.D. It is said the Aos came to chungliyimi at this time and other tribes followed the Aos such as the Lothas, Semas, Rengmas, Angami Chakhesang and the Zeliangrongs and came to their present place at the same time around 1100 A.D. or early 12th century, because their tradition says that the Aos were one of them and went ahead. Whatever the tradition may be, the Nagas came settled in the present Naga Hills in around 13th century A.D.

The allied tribes of the Zeliangrongs are Angami, Chakhesangs, Rengmas and Maos. They were also known as Tenyime which is the combination of five tribes given above and they lived in a compact area.

The Tenyime Naga groups had the same source of traditional dress-they wear a particular type of kilt which is black in colour decorated by rows of white cowries. In Zeliangrong it is known as Nkhim Nai. The women use short Mokhala (wrap over skirt) which comes down to the knec only. This of black colour, decorated by stripes of either red or yellow at the border. The white coloured type is used by both men and women. This is what they called Mareipan in Zeliangrongs dialect.

The Tenyime group also has the same tradition of dragging flat stones to their villages and erecting them as monuments every year. Many of the flat stones were put in front of each house for their resting places in the villages. The whole village is seen with piles of stones which decorate the village with magnificence and dignity. This is not done by other Naga tribal groups.

Formally, the Zeliangrongs were known as Kacha Naga. In the Angami language Katsa means forest. In Manipur, in the list of the Government recognised tribes Zemei and Liangmei were used but in Nagaland they were known as Zeliang. If the Zeliangrongs were unified, those who are in Manipur and Assam will from the greatest and majority group. The estimated population inhabiting Zeliangrong land is round about three lakhs.

3. Background History of Manipur

Manipur lies on the frontier of India. A small state surrounded by ranges of hills, it is one of the beauty spots on the earth and rightly called the jewel of India. "The kingdom of the Indian Rajah, called Manipur State which lies on the border of Burma, is noted for many things. One source gives it credit for having invented the game Polo.[3]" It has even fertile land, located on an upland plateau and is well watered by copious monsoon coming up from the Bay of Bengal. In the hills, which surround the valley, lived numerous Naga tribes to whom the Hindu religion of the Manipuris never appealed.

The early history of here is lost in the midst of antiquity. The history of Manipur prior to 1714 is unknown. So far no authentic record has been found but it is believed that she had been existing as an independent kingdom from very early times. She faced frequent battles with the neighbouring kingdoms of Shar and Pong. The Manipuris were competent horsemen and skillful swordsmen.

The modern history of Manipur starts from the year 1714 when Pamheiba was said to have been shot accidentally while hunting by his adopted father. His adopted father then succeeded him under the name of Garib-Nawas. He occupied the throne for forty years. "He was a Naga boy who was

3. Anderson Bengt : American Baptist Missions Evangelisation of the Nagas (Northern Baptist Seminary, 1956) p. 37.

adopted by the Raj from 1714-1754".[4] A brilliant leader, Manipur assumed under him an aggressive role and in 1754 Garib-Nawas led his last expedition into Burma occupied by his eldest son Chanshah. On their way back, they were attacked by Ajit Shah, one of the younger sons, and were killed. Thus Ajit Shah ascended the throne for five years. Shortly he was driven out by his brother Bharat Shah to die in exile in the Jaintia Hills.

In 1890 Maharajah Seer Chandra Singh was driven out by his two younger brothers Tikendrajit and Kula Chandra. Seer Chandra fled to Brindabon and he sought the British help in India. Thus on March 22, 1891 Mr Quenton, Chief Commissioner of Assam was sent to Manipur with an escort of 400 sepoys. Quenton's plan was to arrest Tikendraj it and Kula Chandra by force. In the early morning of the twenty-fourth, fighting broke out a serious engagement followed throughout the day. In the evening, firing temporarily ceased, both sides agreeing to and the conflict, Tikendrajit invited the Chief Commissioner to meet him. Thus four officers, including Grimwood, entered the fort. It was alleged that Grimwood was fatally speared to death and Quenton and other officers were surrounded and beheaded by the public executioners.

As soon as the news of this event was reached, the British Govetnment of India marched in three columon Manipnr from Kohima, Silchar and Tamu, and captured the two brothers and other officers. The Thangal General, the Rongmei Naga, and others were placed on trial before Maxel' the political agent, and were sentenced to death.

After this event the Government of India offered the moral right of Manipur to exist as a state and notified it in the gazette of India, number 170 E, dated August 21, 1891. Churachand Singh, a boy belonging to a collaterai branch of the Royal

4. B.C. Allen : Naga Hills and Manipur (Imphal) p. 18.

House, was placed on the Gaddi, the throne, and the Political Agent administered the State.

The Manipur Valley was taken over by the Birtish, but the hill areas' considerable tracts remained unadministered. In 1907 the Rajah assumed ruling power and took over from the Political Agent the administration of the state, assisted by a Durbar, consisting of British officers. "Under this British administration the Naga country and the other Assam hill tracts from 'Excluded Areas'—secluded, that is from control of the Provincial legislature and left in the hand of the Governor."[5]

The Land and is Zeliangrong Naga

The Zeliangrong land is situated between Assam, Nagaland and Manipur. It is a mountainous region. They inhabit the compact area of Tamenglong. Churachandpur. Sadar Hills, North Cochar Hills and Nagaland. The Manipur to Halflong sector of the Barail Mountain Range in the east of India is the common homeland of this people. Before thousand years ago they would have occupied upto Lungleh, Lushai Hills (now Mizoram. The ruined ancient relics, stone rows and monoliths are still existing which the Mizos call "Mirong-mun" (meaning the place of the Rongmeis). "Only in the later part of the 17th and 18 centuries when the Kukis began to migrate northward from Chin Hills of Burma, the Zeliangrongs had been forcibly pushed out of their villages and compiled to contend themselves in the present Tamenglong and contiguous area."[6]

The whole country is covered with high hills and mountainous elevation of about 4, 500 ft above sea level. The comprising area is approximatly 5,89 sq. miles. There is a luxurious thick growth of forest. The whole area is ecologically homogeneous

5. U. Graham : Drum behind the hills.
6. M.Z.U. (Manipur ZLR Union) movement submitted to the Prime Minister of India (Tamenglong 1964).

with negligible differences. Due to heavy and continuous rains evergreen vegetation is characteristic of the region. The rainfall is 4017 mm (158,15″). The main products are timber, rice, maize, potatoes, cotton, pan leaves, oranges bamboos etc.

The climate of the country can be divided into two seasons. Rainy season from March to September; Winter season from October to February. March and April experience a few showers with occasional break, and the heavy rain occurs from May upto August. September again has less rain with a prolonged break. Cold winda start blowing by the end of October, and the following three months are very chilly. February to April is the best season and most pleasent with various new sprouts of leaves and flowers decorating the whole area. Though the reasion as a whole is considerably cold, snow is rarely seen, except a little in the morning.

The People and their origin

The origin of Zeliangrong Naga and from where they have come is controversial. They said long, long ago they lived in the MAKHEN of Mao-Maram. The streams of migrating families came down time to time from the northern region, and in the absence of geographical knowledge, they followed the easiest tract of Barak river and began to settle down on both sides of the river and established their permanent home there now called Tamenglong area in Manipur, North Cachar Hills in Assam and Parenten-Taging Sub-Division in Nagaland. T.C. Hudson said, "The Kabui and the Kacha Naga took their origin from Maram. The Kabui Naga are now restricted to the hills immediately north of the Cachar road. There is ample historical evidence and tradition, to show that their expulsion from the hills to the south is comparatively recent.

I have stumbled across ruins of large villages in the jungle, south of Nungba, and learnt that they were the ruins of the Kabui villages that had been destroyed by Kukis or Manipuries in the early part of the last century. There are small villages of Kabuis in the valley of Manipur which are in semi-servile condition."[7]

Colonel M. Cullch also said the following "Songbo tradition gives as the place of their origin, the mountain towards the south of the valley name Thungching. They stated themselves to be at present located on the sites of vaillage at one time occupied by southern tribes who are they said, the elder branch of the family of x which they themselves are the middle and the Manipuries the younger branch."[8]

These theories do not given the evidence for the origin of Zeliangrong Nagas. The Zeliangrong Nagas are the Mongolian stock, and their language was classified under Tibeto—Burmese. All Nagas, whatever the tribes, might have come from the same origion. These are several tribes besides Zeliangrong Nagas such as Thadou Kuki, Chiru, Hmar, Gangte and Vaiphei. The Zeliangrong Naga is the owner of this land.

The Zeliangrong Naga had played a very commendable role of the friend rowards the rising of Manipur who tried to exact tributes from them. During the 18th and 19th centuries in the frequent invasion of Manipur by the Burmese, they gave help to the fleeing Meitei people and their kings from the plain. In Tamenglong village the places called Tunamangphai/Tailamin and Sanari niu where the Meitei families were kept secured for years and such places are in some other villages of Zeliangrong Naga. And it is said that Zeliangrong Naga gave help seven times to fleeing Meitei in several invesions by the neighbouring countries. The Zeliangrong, particularly Rongmeis also entered the Maharaja's service of Manipur and served him. In the Manipur war of 1891 which ended the Independence of Manipur Zeliangrong fought along with the Meiteis. Thangal General,

7. T.C. Hudson : The Nagas Tribes of Manipur : (London 1911) p. 4.
8. Col. M.Cculloch: An account of the Vally of Manipur; (London 1858) p. 14 Rabui is at present known as Rongmei.

one of the heroes belonged to the Zeliangrong tribe. Thus they were allowed to setlle in Imphal by the King. The inflow of Zeliangrongs, particularly Rongmeis in the plain having permanent settled is continuing. The first Christian was the Major of the Maharajah Band who lived at Keisamthong village.

The Zeliangrong Naga Is a composite tribe of four clans : Zemei, Liangmei Rongmei and Mpuimei. They were from the same parents. The question of who was the eldest and the youngest is obscure. As per the custom the youngest son is the heir of the father. As they moved away the eldest son left his parents first and went down to southernmost part upto the boundary of Mizoram. He was the Rongmei. The second son, then left his parents and settled down at the middle part of the southwest. He was the Zemei. The youngest son, who was the heir of the father stayed with his parents on the north where they originated. He is the Liangmei. This movement of migration clearly indicate their chronology to decide upon. The four brothers spoke different dialects but not so different from one another. Somehow they can understand one another fairly well. The root words are the same. Their custom, culture, drees and costume are the same. Their songs are in Liangmei dialect. Their clans like Pamei are found in the Zelei, Liangmei and Mpuimei also like New-mei and Riamei are found. Therefore, Zeliangrong Naga is from the same father. The dialectic differece is due to long seclusion from each other only. The following talks handed down.

It was told that the Zeliangrong people also migrated from Makhei in Mao. They came to Nuimei Mountain now known as Zangkhulen. From there they came to Makuilongdi. The number of the houses were seven thousand, seven hundered and seventy seven (777). From there they moved southward following the Barak River tract. The Liangmei stayed and settled around Makui-Longdi area up to Longdi Pabram and Zemei moved southwest of the Barak river towards North Cachar Halls. The Rongmei followed the tract of the southern

Hemisphere on both sides of the Barak river upto the Mizoram boundary and Tiddim called Doudim in Chin Hill of Burma. A popular song is sung by the Zeliangrong people that Guiremang went down to Tiddim where he established a village called Duidimlong. Guiremang possessed a charm. He was also adventurer. He travelled far and wide. Where ever he passed by or entered any village, girls were drawn and attracted to him. Once when he was in Tiddim area. He fell in love with a Kuki girl. Trouble arouse in the village and he was killed by the Kukis in retaliation to his marriage with the Kuki girl.

The origin of the Zeliangrongs was always stressed on Makhiang (Makhen). From Makhen they moved down in search of land for settlement. They came to Ramting-Kabin a deep narrow cliff of a stream and cave where women and children were left behind safe from enemies. The people went out every day in search of good land for settlement. First they came to a place called Kapung where they lived for some years. From there they moved up to a mountain called Makuilongdi which they chose for establishing a village. By the time they entered the village everyone including women and children came with a stone which they put in one place together. Till now a pile of stone hill remains. Approximately the number of stones would be around twenty three to twenty five thousand. This pile of stones identified that the Zeliangrong people at one time lived in Makuilongdi. The number of the houses was 7777 and this might be true. It was told that the name of the Chief of Makuilongdi was Nguiba.

The Chief of Nguiba had no child. Knowing that there will be no one to inherit him, the villagers brought another girl and gave him for marriage. Nguiba had two wives. In course of time the second wife conceived and got a male child. His name was given as Namgong. Luckily after a year, his first wife also gave birth to a male child and his name was called Kading. After some years again the first wife conceived and bore a male child whose name was called Nrembangbe Nguiba might have got other children incuding girls also but it was not known. Now Namgong, Kading and Nrembangbe, the three brothers lived together for years in Makuilongdi as their father was the Chief of the village.

Now Nguiba became old ; the question as to who would be the heir of his father was aroused. Therefore he called all the elders of the village together to decide which among the three brothers should inherit the father. Some said Namgong, the eldest son from the second wife should be the heir and supported by other villagers. The other suggestion also came that, the first wife's son, Kading was the rightful heir and supported by some. Thus, there were two opinions and two parties were enacted in the village. The decision could not be taken-

Since the decision could not be arrived, the father had to decide for himself. Therefore, he called his two sons-Namgong and Koding together in the morning to him and told them to go to his uncle, Chitu, who was living in Koubru Hill to ask and obtain the opinion as to who should be the heir to his father. His uncle told them to eat and drink and go for rest in the Morung for the might and only in the morning he will tell them. Now his uncle prepared a cow force and a dog for the other (them) and prepared a big chicken curry ready for his two nephews.

In the morning when they came back to their uncle and asked him to tell his decision, he said to them to eat and drink first and will tell about it to them. After eating when they were prepared to go back home, their uncle brought two lunch packets of chicken curry each for them along with a cow and a dog in front of them. He handed over one lunch-packet with a cow to Namgong and another one to Kading with one packet and a dog.

Now when the two were ready to leave his uncle told them, "You should never open the lunch-packet and eat until the cow stopped for drinking water on the way. As soon as the cow drinks water, you should also eat lunch there. By the time you open the lunch-packet, any one in whose packet is found the head of the chicken would be the heir of your father; this is my own judgement between you." He further said, "After your lunch both of you should run in competition and try to arrive your home and the one who reaches home first will be the heir of your father. This is the judgement of God Himself. Wherefore, go now."

After having said all these words Namgong and Kading left their uncle and went away towards their home. They crossed many mountains and rivers but the cow never stopped for drinking water. At last they came to a River called Majaki where the cow went down and drank the water. As advised by their uncle the two brothers also stopped and sat down for lunch. When they opened their own lunch-packet, Kading found the head of the chicken in his packet, Namgong said that according to the advice of their uncle Kading should be the heir of their father. Thus they eat lunch and after which, as told by their uncle, they had to run again competing between themselves on order to reach home first and meet their father.

Taking their animals they started running toward home. In the race Kading arrived home first and Namgong later. Now according to the advice of their uncle, Kading, the first wife's son would become the heir of his father, after his father's death. Thus Kading became the Chief of the Makuilongdi Village and served for many years. The descendants of Kading were known as Liangmei.

After many years, Namgong, the first son of the second wife and his descendants migrated to the South-west of the Barak river and to the North Cachar Hills areas. The descendants of Namgon g were known as Zemei.

Nrembangbe, the second son of the first wife be got many sons and daughters. They moved down to the Southern area in search of land and made settlement on the bank of the Barak river. They even went down to Mizoram boundary in Changphai which the Mizo now call Champhai area. There still remain many ruined Mirongmun (Rongmei Village) in the boundary of Mizoram. They also went up to Tiddim in Burma and once established a village. The descendants of Nrembangbe were known as Rongmei.

After separation, the three brothers, due to long seclusion from one another, became enemies of one another and head-hunting and inter-village feud became common among them. For the same reason their dialects were also slightly different from one another. However, they were not very far from one another. It was understandable when they communicated to one another.

It was also told that the descendants of Chitu, the younger brother of Nguiba, moved down from Koubru Hill to the Valley of Imphal and made their permanent settlement. They were known as Makimei by all Zeliangrong Nagas. The Mao called them Makrimei. Therefore, the Meiteis were the children of Chitu who lived once in Koubru Hill range which runs near Imphal Valley.

The Zeliangron Nagas occupied the large area in North-East India in Nagaland, Manipur and Assam compactly without over-lapping the other Tribal Land.

While stressing the origin of Nagas—where they migrated from, Alemchiba suggested the following :

"The Tibeto-Burmang group probably formed an area of dispersion somewhere in the present province of Sikiang in China, from where they began to spread east and south.....The Assam Burma groups of the Tibeto-Burmans include the Nagas and the Bodos, who came down to Burma and entered Assam and Brahmaputra valley in fairly early times, the Kukis and Chin people who are found in south-east Assam and in Burma and the Kachins or Singphos and the Lotas who has always remained in Burma"[9]

It was commmonly understood and taken for granted that the Naga family in all over North-East were from one stock of race migrated in waves either from China or Vietnam through Burma. They might have lived for sometime in a land where Ocean was very close Because their onrament—necklace etc. were made of the sea-creatures and their shells.

Zeliangrong and Life

The Zeliangrongs live in villages. The site of the village is selected originaly on the high spurs of hills. The village was founded with strict and rigid rules of the customary laws. They have a strong attachment to their villages and lands, and except under extraordinary circumstances, they will not think of leaving their homes. Leaving is regarded degrading to themselves and their ancestors.

The houses are fairly big, respectively showing the importance of the owners. The houses are constructed with wooden posts, split bamboo walls and roof with thatch. The roof almost touches the ground. The front side of the house is high and tapers to thc close end, which looks like the sitting position of a dog. The houses are decorated with 'houses-horoes' (carvings of ancestors) made from the wooden planks. Inside the enclosed verandah, the trophies of the game chase and relics of great feasts such as the buffalo, and mithunhorns are displayed. Even human skulls are displayed, though head-hunting was stopped long ago.

9. Alemchiba : A brief historical account of Nagaland; (Naga Institute of culture, Kohima, Nagaland) p. 3.

Music and Dance

The art of song and dance is an important aspect of Zeliangrong enteratainment. While working in the field, cooking, carrying load, the lips of the girls and boys can be seen rhythmically vibrating with songs, There is no written literature of music and art of dance. But the songs, which have been composed over a thousand years ago by expert musicians like Guiremang, Kariukiu, Asiyang and Hiluwang, are still being sung. The music is correlated with dance as dance is always accompaned by song. The hyms very according to festival, work, war, and sacrifice etc. for all the occasions to be sung individually or in groups. Music and dance are associated with religion according to the cycle of natural agricultural life. The Missionaries who came to North-East India denounced the customary music and dance as devilish. Instead the western music become regular church music. Now almost all the tribals' music and dance are forgotten. It is unfortunate however, that the missionaries were perfectly justified in ruling out the contents of music and dance or the associations of the devilish elements but to do away with the structure of dance is no less than cultural sabotage. Dr. M.M. Thomas says, "The rich resources of the Western Church music should not be kept aside from our people, but at the same time, the rich resources of the tribal indigenous music also should not be left behind."[10] It is good to encourage our church singers and musicians to endeauour to put message to fit into our cultural music to be used in our worship services.

Their dances are divided into various types, festival dance, spear dance, and sacrificial dance. The dances are performed both by men and women. The hands, feet and arms move but not the waist and eyes having more affinity with the Eastern Asian characteristic. This is the friends from the Indian dances.

10. M.M. Thomas and R.W. Tayler : Tribal Awakening (Bangalore 1965) p. 184.

Economic Life

Among the Zeliangrong Nagas begging is practically nil. Agriculture is the main occupation but cultivation is primitive. They adopted the jhum system or shifting cultivation. They go to hills, clear the jungle, burn the patch, plant paddy and other vegetables. In the next year they go to another place. Thus there is a rotation of cultivation in eight to ten years. Each household preserved grains and other vegetables sufficient for each year. Thus the total life depends on cultivation of field only. The rice is the stable food supplemented by other vegetable and meats. The rice bear is the essential ingredient of their every day drink. It is prepared in all houses and stored in big a wooden drum or several gourd-vessels for daily drinking. V. Elwin described it as a nourishing drink as it and stimulating drink. The vitality of the Nagas mostly comes from the this drink as it is the source of energy and strength.

Zeliangrong Nagas are also rich in dresses. It was the tradition that every women from her early life should learn the art of weaving. Cotton is grown in the agricultural field of their own. They dyed the thread with local vegetation and leaves into various colours red, black, neem (blue) and blue. A kind of brownish cotton called Lungzin is also grown and it is said that such kind of cotton is not grown in other countries except in the Zeliangrong areas. The Zeliangrong sense of protocol can be seen in the clothes and shawls they wear. The Zeliagrong Naga has numerous types of different designs of male wears and wome skirts for eifferent age groups which other tribal groups in North-East India do not have. They love to use their own productions only which identify with which tribal groups they belong to.

They have great love for colourful ornaments like ivory, carnelian beads, iron and other fineries. During ceremonial occasions they adorn themselves with head-gear, horn-bill feathers, grand shawls with necklaces and earrings in which he looks like a king. They also manufecture every needful household articles such as baskets, bags in different patterns and desings. They are skillful in cane and bamboo works. Every male member in the family is expected to know the art of making house-hold wares and tools.

The economic life of the Zeliangrongs depends on their labours and resources. They learn and practice how to take care of the need of others. Begging is unknown and nil. "For they know nothing of locks and keys, and indeed have no need of either since the habit of stealing from each other is quite unheard of among these simple people."[11] Whether rich or poor they share with each other in times of need. However poor they may be, they practise good hospitally. The home is open for everyone. If a strangerguest is found or know staying in the village, he will be invited by many families to eat with them. Thus the guest will have to go round to many homes and eat in many homes both in the morning and evening.

Thus the guest knows how to adjust his eating in order to eat in many homes both in the morning and evening. However in this present time the good quality of hospitality observed by each family has gone down considerably and in fact is nil in many cases.

Since the early Missionerarіes forbade vehemently the converts from drinking rice beer and using the traditional dresses which were thought to be unhygienic; the act of drinking and wearing ornaments was prohibited in the church circle till this day. It must be noted that all the bad practices of the old time should be given up and the good ones should be improved. Now to a certain degree change had been made from old to modern—adaptation of western culture which greatly affected the economic life of the people.

11. Elwin, Verrier : The Nagas in the 19th century: (Oxford University press) p. 455.

Speapking of Christian missions in Manipur aJeas Elwin says, "In recent years the adoption of some kinds of western dress is almost as inevitable a token of conversion, Bible reading and singing hymns. In Manipur the Missionaries have insisted on their converts to abandon their traditional ways of dressing hair".[12]

Social Life

The Zeliangrong Nagas social life is grounded in the family, village and Morung. In fact the value of public social life is stronger than individual among the society. The Zeliangrong Naga has joint family system. A house accomodates the man and wife, and his married sons. The joint family system is practised not because of scarcity of land but love of their parents. However, it is not compulsory; it is left to the will of the couple to remain or separate. There are clans and kinsmen such as Pamei/Kamei, Panmei, Gangmei, Gonmei and Thaimei etc. And Pamei, Kamei, Phaomei and Malangmei are alias clans.

The father is the be head of the family and obedience to him is expected from each member. As long as the brothers lived together, the property is jointly owned. In a joint family the eldest son's wife is the head and the granary is kept in her change. A wife after the death of her husband, is she is willing, can marry the deceased husband's brother. But this case is very rare. If she refuses the dowry has to be refunded. And marriage in the same clan is strictly prohibited. It is taboo. If a marriage in the same clan is discovered strict ordeal of the customary rituals has to be observed in order to sanctify them; Only then will they be accepted in the society of the village again.

12. V. Elwin : Nagaland, (Shillong 1961) p. 34.

The Zeliangrong Nagas were head hunters about one hundred year ago. Inter-village feuds, tribal warfare and head-chopping became the religious funtions. This practice continued till the coming of the British rule in Manipur and Nagaland. It was believed that the spirit or the energy, the essence of great power of man stays in his head. If the head is cut off and brought into the village, the head-taker is strengthened with the addition of the spirit of the head. It is also believed that it will increase the fertility of the land and yield more crops. As Chakravorty puts, "Head hunting became the characteristic feature of the Nagas with their inter-tribal feud and fight. All Nagas were head hunters, their women being the chief inceptors to this pursuit as girls would not favour men who had not taken heads or been in a raid"[13]

The whole village is governed by the village Council. The governing system is purely democratic though NUMPOU (founder of the village) has got authority of traditional hereditray rights in the village. Graham Bower says, "Numpou was village priest, the other permanent members, chose elders to sit in the council at any given meeting. But he is not a director. The Council could on occasion over-rule him, if public opinion was overwhelmed behind it".[14]

The members of the Counil is selected from each clan known as Meikhin to be represented in the PEI (Council) of the village. The highest court of the village is known as SHUNGBAM. The Pei is responsible for any case and problem that arises in the village. The case which cannot be decided by Pei, the Shungbum will take up and the final decision is taken there Criminal cases were few. They were simply judged in accordance with the tribal law. Banishment from the village was the usual sentence for criminal and serious offences.

13. B.C. Chakravorty : British relation with the hill tribes of Assam; (Firma Mukhopadhyaya, Calcutta, 1964) p. 13.

14. U.C. Bower : *Drum behind the Hills*, (William Morrow & Co., New York 1950) pp. 78-88.

Morung

The most characteristic feature of Zeliangrong life is the prevalence of Morung system. At least two or more will be found in the village according to the population and size of the village. The boys' club is known as KHUNGCHIU and KAILIU for the girls. Any kind of tribal education and discipline—the art of warfare, handicraft, music and dance, moral and social education are taught in the Morung. The boys and the girls when they reach puberty must go to their respective Morungs and sleep at night there. They organise dance and social work for the whole village.

Bower gives a vivid picture of the young people's education in the Morung, "The system teaches early the meaning of cooperation and responsibility. I have known and employed men trained by both methods of the Morung and the home, and if choice existed, I would choose the Morung graduates everytime. They are of tougher fibre and the rough cornere have been rubbed off. They are more self reliant with common sense and better disciplined, and above all the their loyatly and sense of service to a corporate body is well developed. They have not lost their individualism. They have a view of the world in relation to themselves, a grasp of mutual duties as well vs rights a way of giving a fair deal for a fair deal, which is most refreshing.[15]"

Malunmei

Malunmei is a social instiution of the Zeliangrong people. This is meant for the inmates of Morung (Bachelors, domitory) which plans to hold Malunmei. Out of four Morunge in the viilage any Morung can plan, announce and arrange Malunmei once in a year if the harvest of the year is plentiful and if the circumstances permit them to hold the same. The participants

15. U.G. Bower; *Naga Path*, (John Murry 50 Albemarle St. London) 1950 p. 83.

are of the some Morung and there is no cross Morung participation. The parents of the respective participant will consider whether they should send their son who is the inmate of the Morung holding malunmei, or not. They also decide the length of time they would like to allow their son to participate in it. The participants of malumei will stay in the dormitory and their parents will supply them food at their Morung. They eat, drink and sleep without doing anything. This is to put on weight and to be nourished.

Malunmei is two kinds :

(1) Khungchiu lun

(2) Ra lun.

The first kind of malunmei is the one in which a participant can take part in it for one or less than that whereas the second kind is the one in which any participant of malunmei takes part in it for more than one month and it may extend up to six months and even one year in certain cases. This is very rare and it does not occur in every mulunmei. If one takes part in the second kind of malumei it is taken to be a proud privilege for the participant as well as for the the parents for this shows that the parents are well to do. However, the duration of malunmei for the two kinds differ from village to village. In some villages, if the parents cannot afford to send their son for long duration, they can send their son for malunmei for a short duration even for 4 or 5 days.

Except for Ra lun, malunmei usually starts on the new moon of Ganh Bu and closes at the old moon of the same. And within a month of Ganh Bu the prospective inmates of the Morung can join the malunmei on any day depending upon the length of time the parents decide for their sons. However, the malunmei is closed on the same day for all the participants as fiixed by the Morung within the old moon of Ganh Bu.

The participants of malunmei will join the same on the day their parents went them to participate. On the day of joining the same, the parents will cook chicken and prepare special rice beer for their son. The head of the cooked chicken will be sent for the owner of the morung house. A gourd-full of rice beer also will be brought to the Morung for the use of the porticipants. Other parts of the cooked chicken are distributed to the tunpuis (girls of the clan of the boy) or his tunpuis are invited to taste the cooked chicken. His tunpuis will taste it and bless him. Joining malunmei is known as malun gutmei.

Cooked food and rice beer etc are supplied by the parents of the participants of malumei at their Morung house. A salt cake known as 'Ntei pan' is profusely used throughout malunmei. The Ntei pan is prepared with a paste of rice powder and common salt. The tunpuis of the participants of malunmei will go to the river for baiting prawn etc whenever they get opportunity for the same. The prawn and the fish so caught from the river will be cooked and supplied to their punings (boys of her clan) who are participating in the malunmei.

During the day of malunmei the participants will not go out anywhere. They will not even go to their houses. If they go they will go there holding branches of a kind of spice called 'tamik'. The dried branches of the said spice plant will be burnt to get the aroma and the burning branches will be held by the participants of malunmei while going out of the Morung. When they go out they will cover their heads with shawls. Even when they go out to ease themselves they will hold the burning tamik branches and cover their heads with their shawls. This is said to keep them from the evil eyes or to guard against indigestion.

On the closing day of malunmei, which falls on the beginning of Ngan Ngai festival, the participants are brought out at the village open place (ground) to show the villagers who has put on weight most. The fattest two are selected from among the participants and they are praised and blessed by one of the oldest men of the village representing the village and the Morung. The fattest participant is selected as Luang Thuan that is the Praise of the village and the second fattest participant is selected as Khungchiu Thuan that is the Praise of the Morung. The inmates of the Morung will go the houses of the winners with traditional HUAI KAOMEI. The parents of the winners will give cash or kind to the old man who praised and blessed the winner. This is known as Thuan Keimei. Any of the relatives of the winner may do Thuan Keimei in place of the parents of the parents of the winner There is no fixed amount for Thuan i.e. giving cash or kind for the praise and blesaing Rs 4/- or Rs 5/- is high enough for the same in the olden days and such high amount is given as Thuan only by the well-to-do families.

In other Naga tribes, the malunmei is not practised. This is popularly observed only in the Zeliangrong Society and is carried out every year. This malunmei is the best opportunity and privilege provided for the young people to undergo such system of rules so taht they relax and rest from all busy schedule of toil and tiredness of life from work in the year. It provides ease, enjoyment, peace any serenity in ones' life which help them grow healthy—physically fit and spirituallysound. This kind of relaxation for about 3-6 months in one's life is very necessary. Malunmei is one of the best social life in the Zeliangrong culture we ever come across.

The whole village will ha ve merriment, dancing and singing, eating and drinking on the last day of malunmei. The fattest pig which was reared for years together for the purpose of malunmei was killed for the happy feast on that day. Besides the Thuan (prize) given to the leaders of the village by the first and second winners of the boys, malunmei was a joyous event added to the whole village.

Malunmei is a kind of health competition. R.R. Shimray also stated. "This is typical of the Rongmei, Liangmei and Zemei Nagas. In these communities, there exists a strong urge for good health and long life which everyone of us wishes for but only a few get. Here, at this particular spot of the earth called Tamenglong, West District of Manipur, many people live up to

100 years of age and more. The reason is simple. In addition to the unpolluted air and the freshness of the environment—the mountain vastness, they had a wonderful way of blessing their young ones with good health"[16]

Religious Idea

The Zeliangrong Nagas worship numerous spirtis, Their whole life is centred around the feeling of religion, "The Kaupuis (now called is Rongme) believe in a supreme being who is benevolent. This deity is the creator of the things."[17] They are worshippers of supernatural beings—benevolent and malevolent. RAGUANG is the supreme being who created the world and rules oves it. He also created the firmament and its bodies like the son, moon and stars. He is invisible, but all pervading. He is a good god. They take him to be neutral, and sacrifices are rarely offered in his name because he gives no trouble to man. It would be simply unfair to describe the religious belief of tribal people as onimism. No doubt they worship many spirits, but not that they are superior gods, but that they give disturbances to men therefore they should be pleased by giving sacrifices. Raguang is worshipped so that their souls might go to another world and live.

The spirits are both benevolent and malevolent. They have their separately assigned residences in distinct places and exercise their power within their limitations. The most influential spirits are the spirits of agriculture called Lau-ra. They are offered sacrifices and in turn they are responsible for the care and protection of their cultivation and help bring good yield. The spirit called Nsuang-ra resides in the village, caring and defending the village. He is also given sacrifices sometimes but it not necessary because he is a good spirit.

16. R.R. Shimray : Origin and culture of Nagas; (Samsok Publication, New Delhi 1985) pp. 304-5.

17. Op. Cite. p. 457.

Zeliangrongs believed that the evil spirits are residing in rivers, trees, steep rocky places and dense forests. They have their separately assigned abodes in distinct places and exercise their power within their limitations. The Zeliangrongs also believe that there are eight children of god. They are the heads of the spirit world of benevolence and malevolence in eight-folds with different activities, namely:

1. Koukru
2. Butchaniu
3. Songpra
4. Abum
5. Malatiap
6. Ra-shi
7. Dui-ra
8. Dimei.

These spirits give lots of troubles and mischieves to life of human being. Therefore, they are woshipped and offered sacrifices. Mbiuchaganmei (wild demon) is the most dangerous spirit who can cause a lot of trouble in man's life. So they are ofiered sacrifices so that man will not be disturbed. "After death they say, they go to an underground world, where they are met by their ancestors who introduce them to this new life. It is not remarkable that this some idea prevails throughout all the various Naga races of Manipur."[18]

Life after Death

The Zeliangrongs believe in the existence of the existence of the soul after death. The soul is believed to go to TARUAU-RUM after death. The condition of life after death will be determined by the kind of life he lived on earth. If he lived a bad life on earth, he will inherit a bad life in Taruai-rum. If

18. Op. cite. p. 457.

he lived a good life he will go in peace and happiness to Taruairum. They do not believe in the physical resurrection of the soul. When they were taught about the resurrection in Christ after death, it was more appealing and meaningful to them.

The ancestor worship was not practised among the Zeliangrong Nagas. However, they believe that their soul did not go away too far when they die. It came back and visitrd the home at least the first week and more also. Therefore, they offer rice, curry and rice bear to the soul. This is known as THEIHKUAK KUNMEI or THEIH PAOMEI.

Zeliangrong rebellion

The Manipur Valley was taken over by the British in 1891 with the installation of Sir Churachand Singh on the throne of Manipur. However, the Hill areas, in the considerable tract remained unadministered. "Under British Administration the Naga Country and other Assam Hill-Tract formed, 'Excluded Areas' — excluded that is from the control of the provincial legislature and left in the hand of the Governor."[19]

In 1916 Kukis rebelled in some parts of the hill In Manipur. Though their revolt was primarilp against the British Government, they took the chance while the hills were out of control of settling old scores against the neighbouring Nagas so the Zeliangrong grew restive in their turns, their grudges against the Kukis were many and deep.

On the whole during this revolt the Zeliangrong Nagas suffered very badly at the hands of the Kukis and the Government failed to protect them adequately. As a result they lost their confidence in the Goverdment. Sometime before 1926 a movement was started led by Jaduanang of Kabiron (Puilon) village in Nungba subdivision of Tamenglong District. This

19. U.G. Bower : Naga Path, (John Murry 50 Albemarle St. London: 50).

movement was a combination of politics and religon. It was odd and interesting. For generations there had been a prophecy that "One day a Naga King would arise, drive out the British, and rule over, all who eat from the wooden platter."[20]

In 1929 Jaduang proclaimed himself the promised Messiah. The people became so impressed with him that they began to look upon him as a chosen leader who would overthorw the existing administration, destory the Kukis and the British and and eventually set up "Zeliangrong Raj". The people began to give him tributes out of fear and reverence. This activity was heard of by the authority early but he was not breaking the law so they let him be. However, he was imprisoned for a week in Tamenglong for causing unrest among the Zeliangrongs.

In the course of time four Manipuri (meitei) traders were killed on a trip to Silchar, on the charge that foreigners should not trespass in the land without permission. And he began to emphasise that every man has his own right and should exercise freely in his own territory. Man should not become a slave of others. This activity rose to such a pitch that Commissioner of Naga Hills and Political Agent of Manipur could no longer ignore him. In 1931, a force was sent to capture him. Jaduanang had already left Manipur and entered Cachar where he was arrested by the Cachar authorities. In the meantime the P.A. with the force of Assam Rifles reached Kambiron. They destroyed the temple and idols of the new religion and shot his python to death. The elders of the village were arrested. From there he proceeded towards Cachar where Jaduanang was handed over to him. At Imphal he was tried on several charges and sentenced to be hanged which was carried out on the 13th June 1931.

20. U.G. Bower : Drum behind the hills. (William Marrow & Co.), New York 1950) p. 51.

But the trouble, far from being eradicated, spread over large areas of the Zeliangrongs in Assam, Nagaland and Manipur. The movement gathered strength around Gaidinliu, the Chief disciple, 16 years old girl. She came to be known as RANI by the Nagas. This movement created by her was a very difficult situation for the Govt. Graham Bower says, "Now what the knew two official did not fully form was that Jaduanang and Gaidinliu had been worshipped as gods for the last two years. They had amassed on enormous amount of tributes; and they had secured the allegiance of all Kacha Nagas by proclaiminig the Naga Kingdom and threatening to cast all who refuded to pay and conform. Their progrmme was an attractive one, the very blue print of a Naga heaven—the millenium was at hand, the faithful was to spend everything in the one stupendous feast, massacre the Kukis and live in plenty ever after on their god's miraculous bounty and cash and converts came rolling in. So, too, did crook and gangster In the three tribes, and the girl who faced the Political Agent that day was not only the figure head of as preety a mob as ever graced Chicago, but was herself the hub of money-spinning god-racket. The agent sent her home as too young to go to jail"[21]

By the order of the Government, the operation against the Zeliangrong Movement was launched. The local movement between the villages was strictly prohibited. A number of villages were burent down to ashes, and serious punishment was imposed on the which had been found to encourage the movement. Gaidinliu had just reached the edge of the Angami Naga country. The Kuki caretaker of Lackoma rest house heard of her where-abouts and reported to the Deputy Commissioner, Mr. Mills, at Kohima. In October 1932 the Rani was captured at Pulome in Naga Hills, while they found her sentry drunk. She was tried in Imphal and sentenced to transportation for life.

21. U.G. Bower : Drum behind the Hills, (Willam Morrow & Co. New York 1950) p. 52.

A few days later the whole Zeliangrong area was alighted. This trouble continued to take the from of semi-reigious and semi-martial movement among the people. "At that time the Civil Disobedience movement was going on in different parts of India, and rumour went on that a king called Gandhi, discribed as a son of the famous Jaduanang was coming to rule over after the collapse of the British Government of India."[22]

Many intimate disciples named Masang, Gumco and Dikheo, escaped. In May, 1934 Haido and Dikheo the ring leaders were shot dead. Even after all these the agitation never entirely died out and there were fresh attempt to revive the movement.

In 1937 after accepting the Provincial Self-Government the Congress leader tried for the release of Rani Gaidinliu. But they did not succeed. The Rani was released only after India's independence. Pandit Nehru made the following remarks, "Perhaps she was rather premature that the British Empire still functioned effectively and aggressively and it took vengeance on her and her people. Many villages were burnt and destroyed and this heroic girl was captured and sentenced to transporta tion for life. She lived in some prisons in Assam wasting her bright young womanhood in dark cells and solitude. Six years she has been there; what torment and suppression of spirit they have brought to her who in pride of her youth dared to challenge an Empire."[23]

From time to time the people faced tension and strife both from within and without. The constant political unrest in the area caused the people to realise themselves to be aware in the plan of future political development. Some decades ago in about 1930-34 the farsighted and generous public leaders established the KABUI SAMITY consecrated with the performance, of

22. B.C. Chakravarty : British relation with the Hill tribes of Assam (Calcutta 1964) p. 191.

23. J. Yoy, History of Manipur (Calcutta 1958) p. 153.

CHUKSUAI-GAROUMEI (a customary way of taking pledge of unity and non-enmity). The main objective of this Samity was that any revolution such as perpetual tension of inter-village and inter-tribal war should be abolished. As the organisation was becoming so benefited to maintain peace and order, they felt the need to strengthen the organisation into a wider Samity. So, the elders from three dialective groups—Zemei, Liangmei and Rongmei of Manipur came together and held a meeting at Keishamthong in the capital of Manipur state on the 15th February 1947 decided to form a strong national organisation known as ZELIANGRONG NAGA UNION. The representation were from the three states, Naga Hills, North Cachar Hills, Assam and Manipur. This was the first historical event in the life of the Zeliangrong Nagas. The main purpose was to develop and promote their common interest in political unity, economic upliftment, educational progress and cultural improvement etc. The Government of India also eventually recognised as a political unit who all come under the banner of the *Zeliangrong Council of 1947*.

Both Christains and non-Christians were brought together under this union and shouldered together the common yoke of development and the restoration of peace and tranquility. It also paved the way for Christian evangelists to go about freely from village to village to proclaim the Gospel of Jesus Christ.

In fact, Zeliangrong Area was the most neglected area. This was due to the Political division. They were scattered in three states in the North-East. Thus they became the minority in each state and representation to the State Government was not properly done. Therefore, they were neglected in developmental work. If we look into all Zeliangrong occupied areas in Nagaland, Assam and Manipur there was no proper communication, no proper educational institutions etc. until then and thereby they were lagging behind as compared to other tribal groups in all respects.

Now they themselves realised that improving their standard of life and development in socio-economic and political stability are possible only when they have unity and love. In the same way the Church of Jesus Christ also has been growing steadily in her own strength in the grace of the Lord Jesus Christ. Under such background we see the hand of God helping from behind that will be closely seen in the rest of the chapters of this book.

CHAPTER II

The First Communication of the Gospel Among the Zeliangrongs

Prediction of the Coming of Christianity

Throughout the world, whether they are the followers of Hinduism, Buddhism or Islam, people generally find it very difficult to change from one faith to another. It was so with the Zeliangrong people. To give up the ancient belief which was deeply rooted in their customs or religion was looked upon with hostillity. The good tidings of Christ had to wait till the fulness of the time.

The Zeliangrongs have an interesting tradition about a prophet named Pamei Guibamreiyang of Tamenglong village who foretold the coming of Christianity at least one hundred years before William Pettigrew arrived in Manipur. In a statement which brings to mind Acts 17:6, he predicted a strange future, "the world will be upside down to me". He spoke of roads, markets, shops and fine buildings that would one day be constructed. More important, he had a vision in which he saw the heavens opened with angels moving about and heard bells ringing. Though most of his contemporaries thought him mad, they remembered a song that used to be sung in a strange tune about the bells of heaven. According to this tradition they heard the song sung again years later after Guibamreiyang had died; it was sung by the Christians who called it "Ring the bells of Heaven."[1]

The Zeliangrongs, prior to the coming of Christianity, were bound and blinded by all kinds of superstitions and practices. They were literally dead as far as their spiritual lives were concerned. Living in the dark jungles and forests they were not only far from the touch of civilisation, but also from the true light by which they needed to see the reality of life. While they were living in such darkness, not knowing where to go and what to do, God, out of his love and through his faithful servant, proclaimed the Gospel of salvation in the Zeliangrong land.

Early Missionaries

The British Rule was established with the fall of the resistance of Manipur Rajah against the British in 1891. Along with it, the door for the gospel of Christ was opened. The first seed of the gospel sown in the eastern Gate-way of India was through Rev. William Pettigrew. He was sent out as a missionary by a wealthy English man named Arthington Aborigines whose wealth enabled him to start his own mission programme. While a member of the Church of England, Pettigrew became convinced of the inadequacy of infant baptism and accordingly received believer baptism before he came to Manipur from R. Write Hay, a Baptist Missionary Society Missionary living in Dacca. On his way to Manipur he stayed

1. Down, Fredrick: The mighty works of God : (Christian Literature Centre, Pan Bazar, Gauhati-1, Assam) p. 137.

in Silchar for three years as the power of the British had not been fully established in the State. In this period he mastered both Bengali and Manipuri to a great extent. Mr. Major Wood, the Acting Superintendent of Manipur State, permitted Pettigrew to come to Imphal, the capital of Manipur. Thus he set foot on the soil of Manipur on January 6, 1894. It was a momentous date, for it was then he, the first missionary began fulfilling Christ's last injuntion to His followers to share the good tidings of Jesus Christ.

The primary task with which he began was education. He wrote books to prepare for advancing education and literature such as the Manipuri Primer, Grammer text books and an English-Bengali-Manipuri Dictionary. He soon started two Lower Primary schools at Thangmeiband and terakeithen in Imphal area. As the state authority realised how much the missionary was taking interest in and using his talents for the upliftment of the people he was appointed as an honorary Inspector of schools. At this time the number of schools increased to eleven in the State. He held this office for two years.

Inspite of the valuable services he had rendered to the people, the State of Darbar became jealous of him. They forbade his work which was highly pleading. The State Superintendent had to ask rather unwillingly that he either leaves Imphal or that he stops his missionary work as no preaching was to be permitted among the Hindus of the Meiteis. However, Wiliiam Pettigrew was permitted to work at his own risk among the Nagas in the hills. He went to the North-eastern hills of Imphal, among the Tangkhul Nagas. There he had to repeat the process of learning a language, produced it to print, and prepared text books. Eventually he opened a school at Ukhrul. He also helped the State as an officiating officer in all matters affecting the day-to-day admininistration of the hills. Most of the students who came to Ukhrul from different tribes of different areas became christians while reading in the school. When they returned to their respective homes they helped to spread the Gospel of Christ. Thus the Gospel message was communicated to the Kukis, Anals, Kheis and Maos. However, the Ukhrul School was far away from the Zeliangrong Nagas; there was no possibility for their hearing the name of Christ. They had wait until God found a faithful man to preach to his own people.

As a rule of his mission Board he would go back home after three years of service. But being zealous in serving God, he at once joined the American Baptist Mission which had been at work in the Naga Hills, so that he might serve God in Manipur with no limit of time. This took place in the month of Februrary, 1896.

Because of the increassing needs in the mission field of Manipur, in 1911 Rev and Mrs U.M. Fox came to Manipur. For one year Fox and Pettigrew worked together. When William Pettigrew left for Furlough Rev Fox took complete charge of the mission for five years. He opened the way for higher education by sending the students to high school. He also introduced carpentry school. This new training enabled the simple villagers to make modern furniture and to build more comfortable houses for their own famllies.

The First Convert of the Longmeis Among the Zeliangrong Nagas, Munipur

The first man who found the Lord Jesus was Kamei Namrijinpou commonly called Maipak. He was born at Khoukiu, a village in hills. He and his father moved to the Imphal suburb of Keishamthong, a Rongmei village, following his mother's death. His father secured employment for him in the Rajah's band where he was eventually elevated to the rank of Major. In the course of time he married a girl by the name Pantiguangliu but their marriage was marked by tragedy. All the children born to them died in infancy. In his increasing unhappiness Namrijinpou began to search for some thing that would bring him peace. It was during this time that he met Pettigrew and received from the missionary some tracts and scripture portion in Bengali. He also had long conversations with two of the early Kom converts from Ukhrul School—Teba and Longkhobel. In 1914 he and his wife accepted the new faith. He was baptised by U.M. Fox on the 6th December 1915 in Imphal. In the same year a son was born to them and the son lived. They named him David, alias Kaphunling which means 'the seed of life'. This son grew up to be an outstanding Christian leader.

Namrijinpou and his friends started a small church building at Keishamthong. They began a strong evangelistic programme. Though they were very few, every Sunday they rang the Church bell and worshipped the Lord.

Downs says, "Early in 1926 a church — the second Baptist Church in Manipur was organised by Pettigrew at Keishamthong. Namrijinpou had been only one of the six persons baptised at Imphal in Dec. 1914; others were added to the small Christian commuuity including two Meitei women so that when the Church was established it had 18 members including a Gorkha and a Sema as well as Meitheis, Rongmeis and Kukis."[2]

The hostility of the viilage increased against the family of Namrijinpou, but in spite of this he kept on preaching. Because he was so fascinated by the Word of God, he resigned from his Government position on May 15, 1991, in order to take up evangelistec work among his own people, the Longmeis, in the western hills of Manipur.

At the time when Namrijinpou began preaching, there were some Kuki Christian churches at Tuiyangwaichong, Makui, Taphou and Langkhong. However the Good News had never

2. Op, cite. p. 174.

reached the Zeliangrong Nagas. It is true when Pettigrew said in his report, "The people or Thadou Kukis are on the whole more open minded and acceptable to the Truth of the Gospel than the Naga tribes."[3] We cannot deny the words of T. Luikham when he said, "No one can deny the name 'Savage' for our people with our forefathers naked and their knowledge limited, when they were fighting each other for no lasting benefit and when life and property were insecured."[4] In the midst of such terrible and difficult times Namrijinpou had brought the great joy of peace to his people. Due to his constant preaching, Mr. Jinlakpou of Kaikao Village began to take interest in this new faith.

When the Kukis rebelled in 1918-1919, Namriajinpou's evangelistic work was hampered. The preaching of the Gospel was not possible in the whole areas. William Pettigrew said, "It must not be forgotten the mission work of any kind, so far as the missionaries were concerned, was absolutely forbidden during this local war."[5]

The Nagas began to assist the troop's of the British India against the Kukis. Mr. Rani-kamang Pamei of Dailong, Mr Poudilemang Taothing and Mr Sitonnang Pamei of Tamenglong were the leaders who led the troops and attacked the camp of Laijang (now known as Tamenglong (town) by night and captured Tintong, the chief of the rebelling Kukis. In the south of Tamenglong a troop was led by Jinlakpou of Kaikao village while he was at the outpost of Oinamlong. After a year Jinlakpou was sent to Tamenglong where the Government head quarters had been newly established at the end of 1919. In such a way the Kukis' rebellion was completely subdued.

3. ABM: Report of the Assam (American Baptist Mission, Gauhati, 1913).
4. T. Luikham : A short history of Manipur Baptist Christian : (Ukhrul 1948).
5. Ibid. p. 92.

The First Baptist Church in the Zeliangrong Area

After the Kukis' rebellion an administrative head quarters was set up for Naga Hills Tameglong Branch at Tamenglong (Nrenglongy, called by the local in 1919. But owing to certain inconvenicnce after four years, the site of the head quarters was shifted to a new place about 5 kms southward (at the present site of the present District head quarters). During that time no one from the Tamenglong Village was converted into Christianity except some Kukis Government officials. These Govt. officials and non-Christians of the Tamenglong village constructed a small kutcha house with bamboo roofing for the purpose of worshipping the living God, Jesus Christ, in about 1920 under the initiative of Mr late Ngulhao Thomsong, Nungkhothang and Jalian. Thus, Tamenglong became the village where the first Baptist Church in the Zeliangrong area was established. After the Kuki rebellion Jinlakpou was appointed to an important Govt. post at the newly established sub-divisional head quarters at Tamenglong. There his interest in Christianity was revived through contact with Kuki Christains. He was converted into Christianity and the record of his name of being converted was made first at this newly established Church. Thus, he was the second Christian among the Zeliangrong Nagas. And he was baptised on the 24th Aug. 1923.

Then Mr Jinlikpou wanted to go to his village Kaikao to preach the gospel but since he was in the Govt. service he could not. God provided the way for his servant to be sent on Govt. duty to take a census of the southern part of Tamenglong. While on census duty he preached in his own village. As a result, a total of ten houses, including that of his own family became Christians. Within two years there were twenty Christian families at Kaikao. The village elders of Kaikao complained against the Christians to the Govt. saying that they were destroying the tradition of the people. They ordered the Christians to leave the village. As a result they moved and founded a Christian village which they called Sempang, where they have planted the first Zeliangrong Naga Baptist Church.

When the news was heard by W. Pettigrew, he immediately sent Mr Namrijinpou to them to guide them. Soon a small school was started. Mr Tongul Gangte and Mr Pakho Sitlou were sent to be the teachers. On Sept, 26, 1923, Mr Helkhup, Pastor-in-charge of the North-west area, came and orgainsed them to be a full Baptist Church. And Mr Ladipou was appointed to be the first pastor of the Church of Sempang.

And there is also a tradition concerning the establishment of the Church in the Tamenglong Village. After Namrijnipou had been appointed evangelist for the Zeliangrongs, he visited Tamenglong. The village elders would not even permit him to preach during his first visit. Defying their order he stood in centre of the village and both preached and sang hymns. He attracted a number of children by these activities. For this and other reasons the elders ordered him to be stoned to death. Fortunately he was able to escape. On his second visit, Namrijinpou was not even permitted to enter the village. So he stood outside the village praching, praying, reading from the Bible and singing. Though this visit did not produce any results, the evangelist's words remained in the mind of (a young man named Hurong. Eventually he and a friend named Ngandiyang went to Sempang seeking baptism.

When Hurong and Ngandiyang attempted to preach to the villagers they were driven into the jungles, where they made camp. They continued witnessing in whatever way they could, with the result that they had been joined by five families. A small Christian village was established. In 1930 a church was formally organised at this Tamenglong village.

Persecution

In the early times the Charistians had to undergo severe persecution at the hands of non-Christians. The Christian outlook on society was based mainly on Christian teachings. Consequenty, it was not possible for them to come together in any kind of agreement for peaceful trans action and social function. The heathen counted every conversion as a loss to the old faith. Naturally, the Christians could not comply with the traditional ways of drinking, taking meat which had been offered to evil spirits, worshipping rocks, trees, rivers and observing all the customs which they. were required to keep. The Christians were so impressed by Christ's way of life that they risked their lives to save the new born Christians from being uprooted. They suffered punishment at the heads of the village authorities. T. Luikham rightly said, "False cases were brough against innocent men. When they failed to get their favou rite drinks from the Christians, even the state workers entered into conspiracy with the heathen leaders to persecute the Christians in any way possible."[6]

The village authority of Kaikao knew that the Christians were completely different from them. They began to look upon them as enemies. They complained again t the Christians to the Government that they were destroying the traditions of the people. The Christian had been ordered to leave the village but had refused on the ground that they had a right to remain where their property was. The sub-divisonal officer of Tameng-long aided with the non-Christian elders, ordering the Christians to leave the village within a week, forfeiting any property that they could not carry with them. In addition they fined the Christians Rs. 4000/- apparently for all the troubles they had caused.

In 1951 the Christians of Sempang attempted to move back to Kaikao with tragic consequences. While returning from the site where they were constructing a church building they were attacked. Three Christian leaders were killed and eleven

6. Op. cit. p. 13.

injured. One of those killed was a Jorhat Bible School student named K.G. Jikamang, who was at home on vacation.

Another great hindrance to the progress of Christinity occurred in 1938 when the Christians of Tamenglong proper had started building a house for worship, it was a semi-pucca building. The heathen leaders reported to R.H. Shaw, the then Sub-Divisional officer, Tamenglong, complaining that the building was not of the traditional type. The SDO ordered to destory the building and it came on the 17th November, 1938. A conplaint to the Political Agent of Manipur was unheeded. After the expenditure of a lot of money and labour it was pulled down and rebuilt on another site. Even then the persecution continued in various ways.

R.H. Shaw and the ICS officers particularly were hostile towards the Christians and did everything in their power to prevent its spreading. A story is told about a visit paid by a Govt. officer Mr. Jamkithang, the then Circle Officer, to the Christian village of Sangrungpang. He became extremely angry when the villagers did not entertain him with any rice bear. The Govt. Officers were apparently very fond of it. Mr Jamkithang immediately issued an order that half of the village should give up Christianity and prepare rice beer. Some, out of fear, did so, it is said, but the majority refused. Though action of this kind far exceeded Shaw's authority, hills administrators in those days had great freedom and for all practical purposes could do as they pleased.[7]

The churches also faced a great persecution when the Tribal Cult called 'Harakah' revived after 1948. The history of this goes back to the early movement of Jadonnang and Gaidinliu in 1917. Jadonnang prophesied a kind of Armageddon ln which all the Kukis and British rule would be destroyed.

7. Down, Frederick : The mighty works of God : (Christian Literature Centre, Pan Bazar, Gauhati—1, Assam) p. 137.

For generations there had been a prophecy that 'one day a Naga king would rise, drive out the British and will rute over all who eat from the wooden platter'. Jadonnang proclaimed himself the promised Messiah. After a period of violent rebellion he was arrested and executed on 29th Aug, 1931. His close associate "Rani" Gaidinliu was arrested but released in an act of what turned out to be misplaced chivalry from the point of view of the Govt. in 1948 when India had got independence from the British rule. Following her release the movement was revived. They were an anti-Christian and primitive animistic movement.

In May 1966, four of the church leaders from Namtiram village on their way to attend the Taosem Baptist Church Building dedication, were arrested and asked to curse Christ and follow Harakah, but the Christians refused to do so. At once the faithful Christians were killed.

For about two years the Churches growth wasgreatly hampered. Several villages were burnt down, and several Christians were put to death. However, victory is with Christ. Within the same year 76 families were converted to Christinanity from the same village of Taosem. The churches were growing in the midst of persecution. God was at work while the people were in travail.

Beginning of Christianity Among the Zeliangrong Nagas in Nagaland and Assam

The establishment of the British Govt. in the Naga Hills hastened the spreed of Christianity among the Zeliangrongs by the American Baptist Mission form Kohima. The Kohima Field covered the Angamis, the Zeliangrongs the Chankhesangs, the Maos-Paomeis and the Rengmas.

The Benreu village in the upper Zeliangrong area was the first village where the first church in the Zeliangrong soil was established. The first convert as recorded in the Benreu

Diamond Jubilee of 1981 was Mr. Hezielung, son of Mr. Heluiliswang. He heard the Gospel preached by Neisier, an Angami from the Kohima Village and he accepted Jesus Christ as his personal Saviour in 1897. A record was made by Miss Narola Rivenburge in a journal of the "Star of Naga Hills" that Mr, Heizielung went to Impur (Ao Centre) on foot covering the distance of 100 miles in the hills' road of the Jungle to be baptised by Dr. Rev Rivenburge in 1897. After a gap of eight years two more men were baptised and in 1914 Mr. Heizielung's father and Mrs, Ileuteile, mother of Mr. Namkuheing were baptised at Kohima during the 3rd Kohima Zone Christian Association at Nerhema village by Rev Rivenburge.

Dr. F.S. Downs in his book 'The mighty works of God' recorded that "the first Christian converts were Keneise and Nsangrangbe of Benreu village. They had been evangelised by an Angami. There was a full time Angami evangelist working in the Zeliangrong area. Though the name was not mentioned in 1927 it was reported that a high school graduate was working as an Evangelist"[8].

The uprising of Haipou Jadonnang and Rani Gaidinliu's movements was dawning. The opposition to Christianity was also very strough as the Kampai Cult populalry known as Hraka Worship was spreading throng the Zeliangrong areas particularly among the Zemeis. The recorded number of the Christians was 334 only.

It is important to note that AZ. Guizang the son of Heizielung was the first matriculate among the Zeliangrong Naga community. In 1912 he was sent to Impur to teach in the Impur High School. He served as Head Master there faithfully and died at Impur. He worked as a missionary among the Ao Naga tribe.

8. Down, Frederick; The mighty works of God (CLC, Gauhati, Assam) p. 146-47.

In 1939 AZ. Keneise of Benreu village was ordained for full time Gospel ministry among the Zeliangrongs and he served as an evangelist for many years in the Zeliangrong area. Until 1953, the Zeliangrong churches were included in the Angami Association. The growth of the Churches were very slow due to bad communication. It was reported that in 1951 the number of Christians was 807 only. As the number of Christians increased churches were planted in other villages such as Poilwa, Mpung, Tening and Ntuma etc. The Zeliangrong Baptist Association was established in 1952 with Rev. H.K. Lungalang as the first executive secretary. As the churches grew further, and having had reached other tribal groups like the Kukis, there was a need to form and having fallowship with them. Therefore, they grouped together and established a Zeliangrong-Kuki Baptist Association. However, after carrying on this pattern for some years, the Kukis separated themselves from the Zeliangrongs and formed a separate Association in 1954.

During the Naga Rebellion movement throughout the Naga inhabited areas by the Naga National Council (N.N,C.) for Sovereign Independence, the Zeliangrong Nagas in Nagaland, Manipur and Assam came together and fromed one unit of Army contingency. They travelled widely in their own land in their underground set up. They began to discover for themselves the beautiful land, in which were found rich forests, rivers, valleys and hills, where the Zeliangrong people are living in such compactness in the North east. They discovered as new land with thick forest called Kabeikamning at present known as New Zaluke. This land has been owned by several villages such as Zaluke, Mhainamchi, Samjiuram etc. however they could not utilise the land due to the presence of wild animals, dangerous to human life and at the same time the cllmate was too hot for habitation as well as cultivation. Though the land was fertile it was unexploited for habitation. The Zeliangrong people decided unitedly to come and settle there and established "The Zeliangrong Home Town" there in this valley. Thus the Zeliangrong people from all North East India came to clear the jungles for habithitation and cultivation since the 1960s and the settlement was established. Now the Zaluke valey has been the town of the Zeliangrongs in Nagaland State. This town is one of the most beautiful valley towns at present surrounded by beautiful evergreen trees and flowers and natural hill resorts.

Now the Zeliangrong Zemie. Liangmei. Rongmei and Puimei are livins together in Zaluke valley (Kabeikamning). The churches and the Christian populations are repidly increas-increasing in the Associations. The name of the Association was also changed into "Zeliangrong Baptist Association" (Nagaland). Mr. Bekau Pamei was the second executive secretary of the Association. This Association was running smoothly, comfortably and accomodating all the Zeliangrongs. The membership was reported to be 62 churches with 6000 baptised members and the Christian population was 24280.

Rev A. Visor was appointed the third executive secretary of the Association after he had completed the Zemei Bible translation work and released from the Bible Society of India. Mr. Bekau Pamei has been sent to North Cachar Hills, Assam, among his own people (Zeliangrong) by the Nagaland Missionary Movement in 1986 as a missionary.

During this period some changes have been taking place; the Zeliangrong Baptist Association was changed the Zeliangrong Baptist Council. Now the three dialectic groups for their convenience in growth and administration of the Churches, felt to form their own separate Associationa. Thus the Liangmei group formed the Liangmei Naga Baptist in 1983 and had gone away from the existing Zeliangrong Baptist Churches Council. The Zeme and the Rongmei continued to work together in the ZBCC for some eight years without problem. As the time went by, the Zeme group also felt the need of having their own Association. Therefore, when the ZBCC Annual meeting was held in Febraury 1988, they named themselves as Zeme Baptist Churches Council and the Rongmei group was left alone and thus they were compelled to establish their own Association. The Rongmei Church leaders in Nagaland met together in May 1988 at Dimapur and havc declared and formed their Association known as "The Rongmei Baptist Association", Nagaland.

As the chruches among the Zeliangrongs are growing in Nagaland as well as in Manipur, the need of having fellowship together and maintain their affinity as one Zeliangrong people is very much necessary. God is at work in the minds o the people and they have the sense of love and togetherness in serving the one Lord who called them from the darkness to the light. Though they are separted for their own convenience of communication in their own dialects, they have forgotten their origin, cultural heritage, customs and traditions, songs and music and their affinity to one family which binds them together for deeper fellowship and contributing to a large and wider interest of mission. They are organising a common platform in which all Zeliangrong churches come together for effective ministry of the Lord Jesus Christ. In Manipur, the Zeliangrong brothers and sisters, though they have their own separate Associations, never ignored their identity as one family of Zeiiangrong.

The Liangmei Baptist Association

The Centre is at Tening which has also been the Government centre since the British time. The first Church among the Liangmeis was established at Tening village. And the first convert was Mr Wisong and it was interesting to note that he was born half-blind. He was from a very poor family so that society neglected and looked down on him. Though the world ignored and rejected him God in His mercy and grace picked him up and chose him as His mighty instrument. He heard the love message of God from his neighbouring Kuki evangelist, Mr. Ngulpu. It was sometime in 1927 he accepted Jesus Christ as his personal Saviour. In turn Mr. Wisong constantly preached and witnesssed what the Lord had done for him to many of his friends and the people whomever he could contact in the neighbouring villages. Mr. Adinbou any other friends from Ntuma Village heard the gospel from him and accepted the gospel and became Christians in 1933. As the preaching of the gospel began to expand from place to place, the number of the people who accepted Jesus as their God and Saviour also increased. After Rev Tanquist, the American Missionary for the Angami Baptist Association, Kohima, heard the news of the spreading of the gospel among the Zeliangrong Nagas, he constantly visited and took care of the new fellowship churches from Kohima.

Christianity had been spreading like wild fire, many other tribal groups like the Kukis were also establishing churches, of course, they heard the gospel earlier than the Zeliangrongs. They felt the need of having one Association. Thus in about 1940 the Zeliang Kuki Baptist Association was establised. The Zeme were also included in this Association. Mr. Khongvai Kuki was the first secreatry of the Association. The Tesangke Inspection Bungalow (I.B.) was the first Mission Centre for them. As God allowed and as the time went by, in His will, growth of the Christian population was taking place in almost all the villages. Now the Non-Naga group, the Kukis felt to have of the Association of their own and went away. Thus the name of the Association was changed into Zeliang Baptis Association and they had established their centre at Peren. In 1960 when all the Zeliangrong Tribes—Zeme, Liangmei and Rongmei felt the need of coming together and in order to accomodate in the Association, they again changed the name into Zeliangrong Baptist Churches Association (Nagaland).

As the churches began to grow, the Liangmei group felt the need to from their own Association for their convenience.

Therefore, when the leaders of the Churches met in January 27, 1984, at Kejanglwa village, they dicided to form the Liangmei Baptist Assaciation, Nagaland. Their centre is at Tening town. The Liangmeis have nine Baptist churches with the total Baptist membership of 1500. They are running a Baptist English School at Tening centre. They have four full time workers. Mr. Ramriwang is the first Executive Secretary. They also have one Ordained Pastor and one Licensed Pastor who are leading the ministry of the churches of the Liangmei Christians in Nagaland.

Rongmei Baptist Association

The Rongmei Nagas were in Nagland since the Baritish regime particulary in Kohima and Dimapur. The Rongmeis were in Dimapur since time immemorial and were the first pioneers in making settlement as Nagas. They were called and known as Kabuis by outsiders. This was an adulterated name and was not their original name. There is a small sub-tribe of the Zeliangrongs known as Puimei which was known as Kaupui during British time and thus even at present, the Rongmeis are known as Kabui from Kaupui mistakenly. The Rongmeis are indigeneous people in Nagaland. For the last many years the gospal has not reached them. In very recent years after securing of Statehood in Nagaland, many Naga tribes began to settle in Dimapur and establish churhes which have influenced the Rongmei Nagas to accept Jesus as their Saviour. The Holy Spirit's Revival which swept over Nagaland manipur during 1970's captured the hardened hearts of the Rongmeis and many were converted to Christianity. The first Rongmei Baptist Church was established at Ragailong Village (Burma Camp), Dimapur. The Zeliangrong Baptist Church dominantly Rongmei was also established in Kohima and dedicated in 1982 by Rev. Ramkhun Pamei, Regional Secretary of the Manipur Baptist Convention.

By the time the Zellangrong people from Manipur in mass movement migrated to Kabeikamning in the Zeliangrong area in Nagaland, thousands of Rongmeis also came and settled in the valley, which is now called New Zaluke. This was done with the understanding of all the Zeliangrong peoples, for their own economic development. Socio economic stability, integrity and unity established 'Mini town' for themselves. Now the Government of Nagaland has set up an administrative Centre for the Zeliangrong Nagas. The New Zaluke is one of the fast developing towns in Nagaland.

As stated before, the Zeliangrong churches were one in ZBC under Paren Christian Centre. However, as the people began to grow towards maturity, they were in need of forming their own separate Associations. As Dr. Mc-govran, the pioneer in Church growth study and phiiosophy stated that the basis for Church growth is to concentrate first on the same linguistic and cultural group so that the Church grows faster and firmer. The Chruch is universal. They all will be bound together in Christ at the same time without losing their identity. Forming their own Churches and Associations is the natural growth in which the Spirit of God in their hearts inspired them and worked in them. Therefore, this fact is to be accepted that it is the Lord's will for the Churches. When the Zemei group had taken Peren Centre for themselves and formed their own Association, the left-out groups were compelled to follow the same though they were not in the spirit for forming another Associasion separated from the original one. The Rongmei Baptist Association was formed in Feb 1988 when the Church Leaders met at Regailong Baptist Church and decided to from and organised "The Rongmei Baptist Association, Nagaland". Now the Association is in full swing. The first Executive Secretary is Mr. Meijaolung, a B.D. Graduate from Mahainamchi Baptist Church. They have also appointed the oldest and experienced leader Mr Lallailung to the post of Superintendent Pastor to look after the ecclesiastical management in the

Association. As per report given the Rongmei Baptist Churches in Nagaland was 9 with a total baptised membership of 2100. Due to wide-spreading of the Rongmei Community over all Zeliangrong land in three North-east states of India, they have contacted many other Christian denominational groups, and thus some of the Rongmeis have gone to Roman Catholicism, Seventh Day Adventist and Fundamental Baptist in Zaluke Valley. The total population of Rongmeis in Nagaland was round about 5892 as reported in the memorandum submitted to the Chief Minister of Nagaland, S.C. Jamir.*

The Zeliangrong Nagas are in a way fortunate people. The Lord has provided good land for them, full of evergreen forests, rushing rivers with abundant fishes and hills and valleys with fertile soils. The famous second biggest river called Barak (Ahu Duibak) runs through the middle of the entire land of the Zeliangrong home in North-East India. One of the richest forest named Dungke Forest Reserve is the biggest forest in the Zeliangrong Land in Nagaland. The Zeliangrong people need to come out with proper understanding to fight for the betterment of their living conditions and for the interest of the Nagas as a whole in the Indian Union.

Zeliangrong Nagas in Assam

The Zeliangrong people in Assam of Silchar Valley and in the North Cachar Hills have been living there from time immemorial. They are indigenous people in Assam. Halflong, the present District Head Quarter of North Cachar Hills was the homeland of the Zeliangrong Nagas. They called it 'LONGMANG' which means the Dreamland or Utopia. The Longmang is a beautiful land full of evergreens of the gentle hills' slopes of the forests around. Varieties of colourful flowers on the plateau and running streams of waters adorn it like a mighty Queen. It is a land of case and enjoyability for human

*Memorandum submitted to Shri S.C. Jamir, Chief Minister of Nagaland, Kohima February, 1988.

habitation and settlement. The land is fertile, the climate and weather is moderate throughout the year. The Rail Road link from Lamding-Halflong to Silchar adds beautification and opens up the secluded Zeliangrongs to the national mainstream of India. The name given by a Britisher as Halflong is a distorted one. This is Longmang, the Dreamland.

The Welsh Presbyterian Missionaries entered North Cachar Hills with Gospel of Jesus Christ, but the Zemeis were not receptive to the Gospel in the beginning like other tribals in North-East India. Thus the progress of the reaching of the Gospel and establishment of the Church was very slow. The main rcason among the Zemei was that the converts were allowed to drink local rice beer and observe some local traditions and customary practices though they became Christians. It was reported that the first convert and its Church was established at Malangpeuram among the Zeliangrongs in N.C. Hills. Other tribal groups like the Hmars, Kukis and Biangtes also received the Gospel from the same missionary at the same time. But other tribes went ahead in education and Church expansion than the Zeliangrong Nagas. However, the Lord had not forgotten His people. The Holy Spirit's Revival visited the Zemeis in 1948. Many received the Pentecostal experience of the Holy Spirit's power. They received the gifts of prophecy, speaking in tongues and healing etc. The gospel of Jesus Christ had been carried and spread in almost all the villages. As the Churches grew rapidly after the Revival, they felt the need to from and organise the Zeme Presbyterian Synod. So the Synod was organised and established a Centre in Halflong Town in 1956. Rev Samuel Pame and Rev. K. Kuame were the pioneering leaders among the Zemeis in North Cachar Hills.

In spite of many efforts to evangelise the Zemeis, it was an added problem for evangelists to move about due to strict genna custom of the Village. They did not easily allow strangers to halt overnight in the Village. In any case, the stranger was kept in the Morung for the night which sometimes, of course, gave an opportunity to witness about Christ to the young people at night only. The Zemeis were also anti-Christian as the Zemeis in the N.C. Hills, the stronghold of the Hraka Movement of Rani Gaidinliu. Haipou Jadonang and Rani Gaidinliu's movement for Zeliangrong Naga Independence in 1930s was very strong particularly in North Cachar Hills. This movement was also associated with religious, political, and Social aspects and demanded intergrity. Till recently the Kampai belief (Hraka Cult) founded by them had been still very strong. This movement hampered and hindered the Evangelistic movement and thereby the progress of spreading the Gospel was difficult. Until today 60% of the Zeliangrong population in Cachar areas and N.C. Hills are non-Christians.

In 1978 when the Revival movement broke out in the whole Nagaland and the Zeliangrong Areas in Manipur, the love Gospel of Jesus Christ was carried over to the brothers and sisters of the Zeliangrongs in Assam by their own people. The Tamenlglong Baptist Church, as their Golden Jubilee Mission Project, sent Keirisin Pamei to North Cachar Hills particularly among the Zemeis. This has been carried out with the mutual agreement signed between the Zeme Presbytery Synod and the Tamenglong Baptist Church for mutual mission enterprise in N.C. Hills in 1982. The Agreement Bond is given here.

"The letter from Mr. Mpamei Kadi, Pastor of the Tamenglong Baptist Church was read to the Committee (Zeme Presbytery (N.C. Hills). The Pastor sought active co-operotion from the Zeme Presbytery regarding mass Evangelismtion of the N.E.I. being initiated by Tamenglong Church. The committee took a long time to discuss and deliberate on the matter and it was resolved that :

(1) As an experiment in the inter-church Evongelistic relationship the Missionary from the Tamenglong Baptist Church Mr. MP. Keirisinang be allowed to work in the Zeme Presbytery area. ......

(2) That the new converts should be given free choice to determine which church/denomination they went to affiliate, sheep stealing should not be enouraged at all.

(3) The method of Evangelisation should be Biblically based, and of non-denominational nature.

(4) That mutual consultation regarding the progrees of the work be made at an interval of every four months between the Zeme Presbytery representative and the representative of the Tamenglong Bapt. Church.

(5) That in the case of any confusion arising out of the implementation of the Tamenglong Church project the decision of the Zeme Presbytery or its Executive Committee shall be final and binding.

On behalf of the Tamenglong Church:
Sd/Mpamei A. Kadi, Pastor
Sd/Indiang, Deacon

On behalf of the Zeme Presbytery;
Sd/Rev. Haisamlung, Moderator.
Sd/Rev. K. Kuame, Secy. Zeme Presbytery, N.C. Hills

As per the agreement mentioned above, a great door was opened for communicating the gospel to the brethren, living in Haflong. So, as, an individual, a church, and an organisation, those who have burden for the lost souls also began to preach the Gospel to the zemei Nagas in Haflong. There are more than 55 Zeme villages in Haflong. In these villages there were about 47 Presbyterian churches and 17 Baptist Churches. The majority of the population is heathen. There is still a great responsibility to win them to Christ a Jesus.

Reinforcement of Mission Work

Many preaching groups were organised by the local churches and individuals, who have interest in missions and have burden for lost souls. Mr. DIKAM was supported and sent by a

Government Minister to work as Evangelist Pastor in N.C. Hills particularly at Hangrum Baptist Church. Mr. Guidak Riamei was sent by the Taotep Baptist Church among the Zeme The Evangelistic Fellowship of the Zeliangrong two Evangelists namely, Mr. Kariuchung and Mr. Heudung. The Manipur Baptis Convention Women Society supported Mr. Namziurangbe to work as an Evangelist among the Zeme since 1981. Thus, intensive evangelistic work has been launched in this dark territory of the Zeliangrong. The Nagaland Missionary Movement for 'Reaching the Unreached' project also moved into this area. They are supporting Rev. Bikau Pamei and his family to work in N.C. Hills among the Zeme and Bedo Cachri. They are stationed at Luangmang, Haflong and continue to support the Zemei Baptist Churches and proclaim the Gospel constantly to their own people. The Lord has blessed and granted more souls and have established more churches. As reported by the Evangelist, the number of the Baptist Churches grew to 17. The total Christian population of the Baptist Church was a thousand. The growth of the Baptist Churches among the Zemeis are as given statistically within 5 years span is quoted here.

	Churches		*Baptised Popuiation*
1	2	3	4
1.	Tungze Baptist Church	6	30
2.	Hazeichak	—	25
3.	Koulua (Laisong)	—	68
4.	Hangrum	—	180
5.	Khoukhum	—	89
6.	Duizung	—	25
7.	Baladon	—	20
8.	New Peisa	—	50

(Contd.)

1	2	3	4
9.	Old Peisa	—	150
10.	Asalu	—	I20
11.	Koukang	—	55
12.	Riambanglua	—	I25
13.	Kalulua	—	38
14.	Luangmang (Haflong)	—	15
15.	Mohor (Saron)	—	11
16.	Hanampungua	—	2
17.	Hazeilua	—	12
		Total	1009

The tremandous growth of Baptist Church has been due to the Revival and constant preaching. The Presbyterian Church, on the other hand has also awakened. They began to realise that they are dead and doomed if they continue to drink, and they will never come up to the standard of other abvanced Tribes without reforms. They also began to understand that without having mission vision, their church will never grow as they expected it to be.

Now the Zeliangrongs in Assam and other parts of the North East which have been isolated and secluded from each other for the last many years have begun to re-establish relationship and fellowship among themselves. Better understanding and close interaction with mutual identification has been building again under the one Lordship of our Lord Jesus Christ.

Rongmei in Silchar Valley

The Zeliangrong Nagas liveing in the Silchar Valley area of Assam were many. They live scattered all over the Barak

Valley of Silchar. It was reported by the Evangelists who were constantly travelling and preaching among the Zeliangrong in Assam that they have discovered 41 villages in Silchar Valley alone. The Goapel message had not reched them nor have they heard about Jesus Christ. Even today 99% of them are non-Christians.

Ealier Missionary's Work

Around 1935 some of the American Baptist Missionaries from General Baptist in Mid-America came to India in Silchar, Assam and began to work by establishing school, hospital and leper colonies at Alipur, Lakhipur, Banskandi and Mokundo. Miss Julia A. Rose, an American Baptist Missionary come to Lakhipur in 1936 and established a school where many students who studied began to know Christ as their personal Saviour and become Christians. She helped the Rongmei people in particular in compiling and publishing the Rongmei Hymnal called "Kabui Christian Lu. This served the churches in singing praises to the name of God. She wrote a Primer for the Rongmeis name "Kabungbi" and was also involved in the Rongmei New Testment translation works. Due to her tireless service in typing and readback of the whole Manuscript of the Bible, it could be published and came out in 1979 by the Bible Society of India.

Miss J.A Rose's service for evangelization among the Rongmeis in Assam has been ever remembered by the Churches. She founded the "Kabui Baptist Mission" which centre was at Rosebed, Lakhimpur. Through her effort, the Gospel of Christ has been spread to many Rongmei. Rev. & Mrs Charles Swartz were also sent by the Mid-Mission from America, for the Rongmei Nagas as Missionaries in 1952. Their station was at Binakandi (Ahurang). They established a Bible School there. Though was half lame, with much evangelical zeal he went around in almost all the villages of the Rongmei in Silchar preaching the Gospel. However, the hearts of the Rongmei people were hardened. They could not plant a Church yet among the Rongmeis as they expected.

The Missionaries established hospitals, Christian Literature House, a Baptist Bible College in Silchar. Through all these ministries may of the tribal groups such as the Hmar, Kukis, and the Kachries began to accept Jesus Christ and established Churches. Rev. K. Chunglin Mr. Thiudinang and Rev. Neilalung were among the Rongmeis worthy of record. They were the first leaders of the Christians in Cachar. They went for Theological study in Jorhat Bible School being supported by Miss J.A. Rose and Charles Swartz through the Kabui Baptist Mission. Rev. K. Chunglin is pastoring in Babupara Baptist Church in Jiribam. Rev. Neilalung is teaching in the Silchar Bible College and working as fulltime Secretary of the Fundamental Baptist Fellowship Churches in North East India.

In recent years many Zeliangrong Nagas from the hills of Tamenglong District, Manipur have migrated and settled in the place known as Lungbungjang on the bank of Jiri river in Assam. Those who came from Tamenglong Dist. were all Baptists. It was reported that there about five hundred families settled in Lungbungjang valley.

Three Baptist Churches were established and dedicated in 1987 by Rev. Lanchungrei, Executive Secy. Rongmei Naga Bapt. Assn. selegates from Namdailong, Lungbungjang and Ramgailong Baptist Churches were present at the Dedication cremony. Many men and women were awakened by the power of the Holy Spirit, and accepted Christ as their personal Saviour through the establishment of Baptist Churches activities and missionary work. Still many are yet to be reached and the fruit of their labours are yet to be seen.

The plantation of the Church of Christ among the Zeliangrong Nagas in Assam is a long way to go. The field is ripe for the harvest, but the labourers are few. We need to pray more earnestly that God will send more labourers.

It is a tragedy to know that many of the Zeliangrongs, particularly Rongmies are living in thatch huts along the railway tracks in Silchar. They have no land, no proper shelter to live in, no clothes to wear and no food to eat. They earn and live as railway labourers. Many families sleep on the railway's platfrom. Now, they need to be given proper rehabiliation and settlement in a proper land. They need to be given proper education and care. Above all, they need to be given the Gospel, particularly the Zemes in North Cachar Hills. They need to be rescued and be kept in safe place and be restored to their normal lives. The Churches of the Zeliangrong in North East India should need to come together by shedding their own identity as Zeme, Liangmei, Rongmei and Puimei and from a strong unit of Baptist Organization covering the whole North East India and thereby the Lord's will can be fulfilled. The children of Israel, the 12 Tribes were from one ancestor i.e. Abraham, Issac and Jacob. They became the chosen nation of God. They were chosen by God to be the example of God's love. His interest in the their affairs is to show His love in the world through Israel. Similarly, the tribes of the Zeliangaong- Zemei, Liangmei, Rongmei and Puimei were from the one father of *Nuimei* and *Ramtingkabin*. God has chosen the Zeliangrong people to live an occupy compact area and the best land in North East India. We must be grateful to God for what He has done for them. God in His son Jesus Christ has shown the way of life, eternal salvatlon to His people. It was not because the Zeliangrong were righteous, but in mercy, in His son Jesus Christ, has chosen the people of Zeliadgrong to establish His Churcn for His mighty service. As Jesus said to His disciples in His great commandment and mission" Go and preach to all nations ... I will be with you to the end of the age." (Mathew 28:18). If we obey His commandment, the Lord will with us. If the Lord is with us nothing will be impossible. Let us fight together for the cause of the Gospel. We are one family, in love let us serve Him together that we will be known as His disciples.

Revival

The severe persecution acted as a strong stimulent to serve God and stood for Christ with re-inforced zeal. The Christians called on God, their father, for help. Like a wild fire the great revival swept over the areas. They were filled with the Holy Spirit and even prophesied as in the day of the Pentacost. They saw visions of heaven. For a month they spent their time in prayer, meditation and singing as if waiting for the immediate coming of Christ. People around them called these Christians drunkards and mad men. God responded to their entreaties and gaxe living water to ease the aching hearts of suffering people. This revival first started from the Baptist Church Sempang in the Zeliangrong area.

The immediate result of the revival reached many villages. The Sampang Baptist Church had established a school and an orphanage where students were invited to study free of cost. Mr. Latdi and Hulenang were employed as special evangelists to tell the Good News to unreached villages. They faced much hardship and persecution since in those days the strangers could not come and go freely from village to village, due to inter-tribal feud war. They slept in the jungles without food and clothes. Prayer and dedication, faith in Christ were their daily food. Due to their constant preaching, strong Churches were established in Sangrungpang and Taobam in 1924 and 1926 respectively.

Following the revival Dr. Crozier gave a report in the Missinary meeting, "The present Church membership is 437, the cash contribution of the Churches is Rs. 279-14-9 during the year."[9]

The Gospel message had reached the villages of Banrong, Tamenglong, Saram and Panrong and the Churches were organised within four years from 1925-1929. These decades bore the seed of revival greater than any before. Thus the cause for

9. Op. cit. (1972) p. 62.

which the Christians had suffered so much came to be vindiated.

The spiritual Revival Movement started in Manipur about 29 years after the coming of Christianity in Manipur, and after about 15 years in the Zeliangrong Churches. This movement broke out at Sempang Church, in the South Aling Nsan Church and Makui Church in the North. Those churches were also blessed with many spiritual gifts of seeing vision, prophecy, speaking in strange tongues etc. but due to ignorance and lack of guidance revival could not spread to other parts of the Zeliangrong area. This revival movement was believed to have started and spread from the Lushai Mizo, who at that same time received the revival fire from the Welsh Revival movement, started in 1904. The revival movement started in Mizoram for the third time and from this very movement the then revival in the Zeliangrong Churches received this revival. "The third revival which had been occuring on the 26th July, 1919 simultaneously both in the north and in the south...."[10]

Revival in the whole Zeliangrong Area

The recent revival movement is the third revival movement in the Zeliangrong area spread out from Nagaland. Several Bible classes and trainings were conducted in the Churches before this movement. It was in January 1975 that a Gospel Campaign led by Rev. Subodh Sahu was conducted at Tameng-long town Baptist Church and also in the first week of December 1977, a Gospel Crusade called "Salin Crusade" was conducted at Tamenglong Town sponsored by the Zeliangrong Evangelistic Fellowship. Many people from the different villages of the area attended the two meetings and it was in these two meetings that the people had the desire to have the spiritual revival, movement. When the leaders saw the keenness of the people for having the spiritual revival, they conducted a Revival

10. J.V. Hluna. Church and Politics Upheaval in Mizoram, p. 25,

Crusade at Tamenglong village Baptist Church under the theme of "Ye shall receive power....Holy Ghost is come upon you." Acts 1 : 8 during 4th-9th April 1978. The overall arrangements of the Crusade was made only within 2/3 months but the Churches of the surrounding area made a good response and the Crusade turned out to be the most blessed and joyous crusade ever held in the Zeliangrong area. In such services ten to twelve thousand people attended daily.

It was also the most crowded Crusade in the area. About 60 counsellors including the spekers of the Crusade from Nagaland came and helped in conducting the Crusade. Six to eight thousand people attended everyday. God worked in a miraculous way during the Crusade. Many received the forgiveness of sins, many broken homes were restored and many Church leaders rededicated their lives to Christ. Whenever people get together, that place turned out to be the place of worship and praise. God in His mercy lifted the minds of the poeple and the talk of the people during that time was only about the saving grace of Jesus Christ and the songs that people sang were only about the redeeming blood of Christ. The people began to sing in every place whether at work or at rest and it is indeed a strange experience to note that the songs they sang came out spontaneously even before they intended to sing. Singing of revival songs had such an influence that even the non-christians also learned, familiarised and sang these spiritual songs with keen interest.

Seeing of visions, prophesying of the work of God and speaking in tongues were the very phenomena by which the whole church members in the Zeliangrong areas were alighted to a deep spiritual conviction and commitment to the task of the Cospel. Healing of the sick and many disease were common; like in the day of Jesus, many deaf, dumb and paralytic were healed. The author himself experienced a number of instances. Once a Revival Crusade was conducted in Puichi Baptist Church when an old lady about 80 years old who was blind and deaf, after offering of prayer with singing by standing around her, recovered completely a nd even came to attend the evening worship service.

Outcome of Revival

On seeing the great works of God, Satan also tried to bring utter confusion among the people. There were confusions is the Churches and even among the Church leaders. Leaders started politicalising even in the Church administration. In some cases, people began to depend only on vision, prophecy, trance, unknown tongue etc not depending on what is written in the Bible. They depended only on emotional and individual experiences that shouting, clapping and weeping were the signs of spirituality. Inspite of all these confusions, there were also great progress in the Zeliangrong churches, through the Bible by the Church leaders.

The believers were encouraged by conducting several programmes in different areas and churches. They had the burden for the lost souls and believers started preaching and teaching the gospel around them. Many were converted and many were added to the Churches. Faith of the people increased tremendously. Number of the churches also increased; many church buildings were expanded and in every church there has been tremendous progrees. Giving and offering for the Lord's ministry increased. Many young people came out full-time ministry. Many were sent for theological training. There were blessed to become high ranking government officers. There were great changes in physical and spiritual development of the churches.

The Zeliangrong people have really witnessed and experienced that people have the real light when the gospel of Christ came to this area. "The entrance of Thy words giveth light." Psa. 119 : 130.

Outcome of Revival Continues

During meditation and earnest prayer, many saw strange visions and went on trance for 3 days. Once, a lady, Mrs Dizinliu, of Tameglong village went on trance for 3 days 3 nights. She was taken to Heaven and was shown the horrible scene of hell where thousands of people who did not obey the Lord were tormented with anguish and shouted for help but were utterly helpless. She was also shown the beautiful heaven where the dear ones who knew the Lord went to be with the Lord in joy, peace and bliss. This happened in 1978 when a great Revival swept throughout Zeliangrong areas in the North-East India. She was also shown by the Lord that those commited their lives and have backslidden will be given severe judgment by the Lord. The similar nature of judgement upon the wicked people and unbelievers that would happen were also foretold. Many other people like Mr Dinthuiyang, the ex-Superintendent Pastor of ZBA who served the Zeliangrongs and retired after 55 years of service, also saw a vision; along with him Mr Kaigongpou, Mr. Thomraibou and Mr Disimremang, Mr Chongloungam were called by God to go to all corners of the Zeliangrong areas and to encourage and teach the word of God. Among the ladies, it is worth-while to mention Mrs Ganangpuangliu Mrs Alu, Mrs Japamgoliu and Mrs Kandokliu who went about in all the places of N.C. Hills, Silchar Valley and to the families particularly in Imphal Valley, Manipur. They constrantly preached and healed the sick and thereby many hard-hearted souls were won to Christ. Thirty-nine churches were established in Imphal Valley among the Rongmei Nagas only.

The cold hearts were melted; the dead souls were made alive. The hidden corrupted minds were opened, made to confess and repent of their sins. Many who were under the bondage of Satan were released. Once 1989 in the month of October, in the village of Noney (Longmai) a young man called Enoch was possessed by the devil. He was uncontrollable; he went about with the dao and spear; triend to hurt any one whom he met. He was chained with a big iron chain; his hands and feet were bound on two posts as if crucified. He was bound and tired there for weeks together as there was none to dared to approach him. Mr. Namnethuan Palmei and his band of praying members went to Noney and they prayed for him; immediately the devil who was torturing him left him. He came back to his right senses and came to the Christian Centre, Khongjaron in October 28, 1989 and gave his testimony while the Zeliangrong Missionaries Training was on session in which the author was one of the Teachers and witnessed his testimony in an open public worship meeting. The Lord's power is much greater than Satan's. The evil one can never thwart the power of God.

Once in November 27, 1989 at Namdailong Baptist Church. Lungbungjang, Assam, a great miracle happened. There was a man named Namjuan who fell down from a high tree and broke his abdomen and waist. The whole lower parts of his body became paralysed and could not walk. His legs were dried up. The urinal passage was disordered. Without consciousness, his urine was dropping continously. The passing of his stool had no limitation; it passed out at any moment. He was in the Alipur Christian Hospital for one complete year. There was no improvement. He had been suffering terribly. He wanted to be a christian but he never knew what a church was and worshipping God was. While we were having a Bible Camp at the Church of Namdailong, we were asked to come to his home and pray for him. As we entered the house we saw him sitting without stopping the passing of urine. The whole room was filled with bad smell. He just sits, works and talks. We told him to repent of his sins. He said, "I do not know what things to say" We prayed for him to confess the wrong deed he had done to the Lord Jesus Christ. We prayed for him three times; immediately the urine stopped flowing. We praised the Name of Jesus for healing him. He was asked to get up; we asked him to praise the name of Jesus shouting "Hallelujah" ! On the following day he came to the Church service and gave his testimony before the congregation. Though suffered under this bondage of sickness for the last three years, now he was set free and was healed physically and spiritually.

In the same village a house-wife lost her three chickens three weeks. back. They never retuned. One buffalo was injured on the head and flies laid eggs on it and it suffered terribly. We were asked to pray. The Lord answered our prayer. On the following morning all the missing chickens came back; the buffalo was healed. Our good Lord cares not only for persons but even for the cattle and all the properties belonging to His children.

The whole Zeliangrong Churches were alighted and awakened by the Spirit of God. As in the days of the Apostles, whereever the Lord led, they went and preached and witnessed the wonderful mighty works and loving concern of the Lord Jesus Christ to His people in the Zeliangrong Area in the North-east and a round. They encouraged, admonished and ministered with the Word of God and thereby experienced the wonderful acts of the Holy Spirit's power. It was also reported that in 1978 the whole year, in the civil Hospital of Tamenglong District, there was not a single patient admitted except one or two police/military personnels. It was also said that in the village of Tamenglong, in the year 1979 not a single death occurred and no funeral service was conducted by the pastor. The whole area was experiencing peace, happiness and prosperity. There were no incidence of theft. There were no drunkards and smokers and other social evils. It was the year of peace, calm and tranquility. The Holy Spirit Revival has been the work of God and was given to His churches to proclaim that Jesus Christ is the Living Saviour,

The Revival produced the following effects in the life of the Church, the whole community and individual.

1. *Conviction of Sin*

There is one thing that is always prominent in the genuine Revivals of the past days, viz, a deep and true conviction of sin. Where there is genuine conviction of sin It is not necessary to urge or pressurise sinners to repent; sinners will come out of their own accord—without being forced. Those who go home from the meeting were unable to eat or sleep because of deep conviction. They prayed and were anguished throughout the night, confessing sins after he has committed in his life. They came with hearts bowed down, broken and contrite with the cry of guilt-laden soul, "God be merciful to me a sinner"; trembling with the burning question of life and death of Philippian jailor, "What must I do to be saved?" Thus God prepared the ground, the Holy Spirit convicted sins before men can truly believe. Thousands came forward committing their lives for God service.

As Chas, C. Finny said, "A revival always includes conviction of sin on the part of the Church. Back-slidden professors cannot wake up and begin right away in the service of God without deep searching of heart. The fountains of sins need to be broken up. In a true revival, Christians are always brought under such conviction; they see their sins in such a light that often they find impossible to maintain a hope of their acceptance with God. It does not always go to that extent, deep cenviction of sin, and after case of abandoning all hope."

2. *Judgement*

When there is revival, there is judgement as well as Salvation. It was discovered that when men deliberately oppose and rebel against the work of the Spirit of God in their community, God often strikes them down in judgement, sometimes with death as case of Hnanias and Sapphira. Once a pastor opposed revival and left his pastorship and backalidded, indulged in drinking and gambling. His wife gave birth to a child, dead, without legs and hands. It was a shock to the family. Second time a baby was born, alive, but without hands and legs. As it was horrible and terrifying to the family they secretly killed the baby and buried him. Before long, one day his wife went out to the field to collect vegetables. On the way she was raped by some gundas and they murdered her and left the body under the tree. Once a married wife opposed Revival and did business in drugs and ganja. She hired a car and came to the town with a car-load of Phensidyle bottles for sale to young people. It was midnight at about 11 a.m. Suddenly, from above the road, a big stone dropped down and smashed the car and her boyfriend at the spot. It was a clear midnight; there was no mark or spot of stone being rolled. So striking was God's judgement. God uses judement as well as salvation in days of Revival,

3. *Amazing Result*

The Churches, individuals, Government officers, contractors were greatly awakened to the mission. The Churches were thronged to capacity. There was no need to spend money on expensive advertisement in order to make the services known. The churches were automatically filled. They were packed to capacity. Everyone was interested in Revival. Religion had become the main topic of conversation, not politics but religion and God. Everyone smiled and was happy. The rich and poor, children and adults, drunkards, the intelligentsia, scholars, leaders of society, all classes were reached and influenced by the power of the Holy Spirit. Most of the leaders of the society were affected and ***brought to the Lord Jesus Christ.*** Restitution was made, debts were paid and obligations met, court cases were compromised, disputes or land cases were settled Whenever there is genuine revival things are made right among fellowmen.

In every revival there must be restitution or else the revival is not genuine. Restitution is one of the natural results of the movement of the Spirit of God upon the community. Revival brings apologies and reconciliations.

Another wonderful result was the recruiting of men and women for the ministry and the mission field. Those who were in Government service resigned and became full-time evangelists. Mr Kameichung of Rangjan village, Mr R.K. Dikau of Tamenglong village and Mr Thuankubui Pamei of Khumji, who are actively working in the Mission field showed the great example. There were young men and women who undertook Theological study and enrolled for full-time ministry. Where there is no revival, it is difficult to get people to enter the ministry or to go to the Mission Field. It was due to the Revival's inspiration that the income of the church was increased and doubled. Those who never attended church and gave tithes were inspired to attend the church and listen to the Word of God; the church attendance became regular. It is the Spirit of God who is at work in a special way in the Revival. The Tamenglong Baptist Church income was doubled to more than two lakhs. Clapping, dancing and singing loudly, shouting 'Hallelujah is not the only phenomenon of the Revival. The flame burning and warinng the cold hearts uplifted men and women to deepen their faith and to commit their lives to the ministry of our Lord Jesus Christ. Whenever the Spirit of God is at work men come forth with increased zeal for the Lord's service.

4. *Traivailing in Prayer*

Revival resulted in traivailing in prayer and is of paramount importance. People spent time in reading the Bible and prayer. Fasting prayers were organised in community in the church for individuals and families. Each family regularly spent time in prayer and devotion. Old people's groups, women's groups fixed date and time every week and spent much time in prayer People spent two to three days, even a week in fasting and prayer. As a result, God came down in mighty power and without any invitation or coaxing, men and women found their way to commit their lives and gave themselves to the Lord Jesus Christ.

5 *Eagerness in Evangelism*

A genuine Revival resulted in the churches and individual's call to Evangelism. The burden for brining lost souls to Christ came on headway. The Zeliangrong Evangelistic Fellowship was organised, and began to send missionaries to N.C, Hills and Assam. Some individual officers and contractors also sponsored evangelists and sent them to various places in Imphal Valley and around. Taiphai Rongmei Evangelistical Fellowship was organised. Zeliangrong Evangelistic Movement of the ZBCC was functioning. The revival brought a big wave of mission outreach to the unreached. Revival without mission and Evangelism is not a real revival.

6. *The Living Standard, the Awareness of their own Situation was Raised and Created Unity*

The Zeliangrongs were illiterate, backward and poor. They were ignorant and had no knowledge and understanding about what was to be done for their situation. For years togeher they lived and practised what their forefathers had laid down whether good or bad. When the Revival swept into the land, a new wave of inspiration sprang up; their mind were enlight ened; their eyes were opened. They were awakened and alerted with the message of God. Everyone began to be conscious of their position and environment in the family, society and churches. They began to see things differently for their future perspectives. The living standard and the economic status were raised. It was a common talk now that the era before Revival is one and lives of the people after Revival is another. Revival brings unity and strengthans the churches. Bringing division, quarreling, disputes and confusions in the name of revival is wrong. Such types are not genuine Revivals.

7. *Social, Economic and Political Awareness*

The Gospel of Christ gives light to the darkness. The mind of Christ gives wisdom to choose what is good and evil. As in the days of the apostles when the believers were scattered in all directions (North-South-East and West) for preaching and witnessing, they began to see and understand each other's needs. The Zeliangrongs began to be conscious and understand their Zeliangrong situation in the different states of the North-East region of India. They felt the need for unity and integrity. They collected relief and gave to those who lived in poverty particularly in N.C. Hills. The Zeliangrong Peoples Convention had been organised. They made several trips to New Delhi and began to move the Government demanding their rightful claim for bringing political unity of the Zeliangrong Nagas in the North-East.

The Zeliangrong Church Leaders coming together from the three states in Fellowship organised and began to move for unity and serving the Lord in one accord.

The genuine Revival really brought amazing result for much emphasis was placed on the preaching of the Word. The seriousness in religious activities paved the way in the mind to centre around in preaching on *sins. salvation, Heaven, Hell and Judgement*. These five subjects of course, must be proclaimed. Therefore telling about Heaven, warning about Hell and dealing about eternity is Scriptural. Last of all, Judgemsnt. People must be brought face to face with the judgement of the Almighty God. They must know that God has appointed a day in which He will judge the world, and that one of these days they will have to stand before their creator and be judged. When this tremendous truth of the Word of God was brought to bear upon the people, a new chapter and history in the human race was experienced. The whole Zeliangrong countries have been alighted with the flame of Revival in the power of the Holy Spirit.

Oswald J. Smith strongly said that there are two ways to work ; "We can carry on our work if we want to in the energy

Smith, O.J.—The passion for Soul Marshal Morgan and Scott. p. 136.

of the flesh which does not require passion, burden or travail. It simply requires gifts, talents, organisation, machinery, education and training. What we are doing is on His Word. What God does say is 'Not by might, nor by power, but by my Spirit (Zechariah 4:6). Revival is not by human ingenuity, not by machinery, not by organisation but by the dower of the Holy Ghost. "There is a peculiar mysterious atmosphere that falls when there is genuine revival in the power of the Spirit. But it is absent when one is ministering in the energy of the flesh. Therefore Spiritual men will be able to discern between the two.

The Zeliangrong Baptist Church need continuous Revival—the outflowing of the power of the Holy Spirit for deeper commitment in the faith and stronger in the mission and evan gelistic work in reaching the unreached before the end of time comes.

Kangpokpi Mission Centre

During the First World, War a great need for a labour corps was felt. Rev. William Pettigrew was requested by the Government to persude the hill people to provide the contingent to go to France. The unwilling tribes came to realise their obligation to the British Govt. in such crisis. Many Christian workers and students came forward. By this act the prestige of Christians was raised and the confidence of the state greatly enhanced. William Pettigrew served as a captain in the army in India.

When Pettigrew came back from war, he pleaded strongly for a piece of land for the mission work in Manipur. It was because of Pettigrew's war service that the Govt gave permission for a second missionary family to work in Manipur. During the years of Kuki rebellion, Dr. Crozier served as a Govt. Medical Officer. In appreciation, for the services rendered the mission was finally given permission to purchase land for a new centre at Kangpokpi on the Imphal-Kohima Road. In 1919, the year during which Pettigrew left for Furlough, land clearing and building began at Kangpoki. In November Dr. Crozier moved to the new centre and were joined by the Pettigrews in 1921. A middle Middle English School, an Orphanage, a leper asylum (the first in Manipur), and a dispensary were established.

Kangpokpi was conveniently located for communication of the Gospel for the whole area of Manipur, the centre of Ukhrul was moved there. Following the opening of the centre, the work of the missions was divided between the two missionaries. William Pettigrew was in-charge of the schools and of the North-East and Sadar area. Dr. Crozier assumed responsibility of the dispensary, the leper asylum and the North-West area.

The mission work in Kangpokpi was continuing in full swing The dispensary was converted into a hospital and the M.E. School was closed down in 1953; replaced by a Bible Institute now called Manipur Theological College. It was though the hospital that many received healing for their bodily sicknesses. It was through the ministry of the Bible School that sick souls were awakened to a new way of life and enlightened by the light of Christ.

CHAPTER III

Education in the Early Mission

Christian Schools

Education was the primary important work of the missionaries as a means of propagation of the Gospel of Christ among the Hill tribes. William Pettigrew started a school in Imphal but the Raja objected. He went to the Eastern Hills of Manipur and began another school at Ukhrul in 1896. As Ukhrul was far away for the Zeliangrongs none could go to study there. In 1920 Dr. Crozier opened a Middle English school at Kangpokpi which according to American standards would be 8th grade. Some of the Zeliangrong boys—Buising, Phenri, Kiulengpou and others studied at Kangpokpi Mission School. These students became the leaders of the church. Practically all the early converts were won to Christ through education.

In 1925 the first school for the Zeliangrong was established at Sempang and along with it an orphanage. The Zeliangrong Nagas began to see the light of education and began to feel the presence of missions among themselves through education.

Realising the important of education in communicating: he Gospel, primary schools were opened by churches in every Christian village. The teachers were appointed by the Association. They were teacher preachers looking after the village school and also helped the pastoral care of the congregation. They were paid by the village church.

Besides the village Christian schools, the association also maintained three lower primary schools at Sempang, Thangal and Saramba. The schools were run up to the time when India got Independence in 1947. Teachers were Boudiyang, Laokeinang and Dijinang respectively. There were altogether twenty schools including the Association schools in the Zeliangrong area. Mr. Phenri was employed as an inspector of the mission schools. The Bible and hymns were taught in the schools. The mission schools served a vital function in the life of the church in communicating the gospel. These schools were indeed the cornerstone for spreading the Gospel.

The achievement of Independense for India created an entirely new situation for mission schools. Secular education rapidly spread in all sections of the hill tribes. All the church schools were closed and converted into Government schools. Though unfortunate the Church felt very much financially relieved as the management of the school was taken over by the Government. In the Government schools there was no longer place for scripture lesson and hymns which were essential part for the growth of a christian life.

Now a good Church school would be essential to effectively communicate the Gospel of Christ to our young generations. The secular education of the Government was not in a position to provide education in respect of moral life. Most of our young people were led astray by modern secular trends.

In realisation of this fact, a Christian Model English School was founded at Tamenglong in 1967 by a group of devoted Christians. There have been more than hundred students admitted each year. The School is fully supported by the Zeliangrong Association knowing that the young boys and girls could be reached when there is religious instruction in the Church school. This school has fulfilled the desire of the people that the younger generation might know better what their lives in Christ mean, The second important school was established by the Zeliangrong Evangelical Fellowship known as United Baptist School. This name has been changed to "United Builders School" now. This School has been recognised by the Zeliangrong Baptist Association and was given assistance towards its development. More than six hundred students were enrolled in the school every year. Christian discipline and spiritual environment were provided in the School. Scripture was also taught in each class.

Realising the importance of the Educational institutions for mission work more schools were opened like Seven Sisters School, Brighter English School, Pretty Lamb Institute etc. The Roman Catholic Church has also established a school in a big set-up at Tamenglong. This is called Don Bosco School. A thousand students are studying bearing good reputation.

For the extension of the Kingdom of Christ on earth, education is the foundation and root for the tribal and particularly for the Zeliangrong Nagas. They are still behind the rest of the other tribal groups in the North-East India. Therefore education must be the first priority of the mission of our Church. All born children should be sent to good school where mission and Christian orientation is practised. Realising this important need the CASA (Church Auxiliary for Social Action) has also started construcing a school at Christian centre, Khongjaron, costing more than eight lakhs rupees for the whole Zeliangrong community. Hopefully anticipating to start class by 1989. This is the joint project school of the Zeliangrong Baptist Churches.

While dealing with the work of education, we cannot ignore the work of the Sunday School. The Sunday Schools were the main structure in educating the people in the light of Christ. The Sunday Schools were organised in all churches. The study of the Bible was emphasised for all the members of the Church. And all the members of the Church attend Sunday School, and every member from the young children to the grand-parents are enrolled in the classes.

The Zeliangrong Association has employed a promoter who takes responsibility for the improvement of the Sunday School. The Association prepares lessons for the schools and conducts examination for all grades. They are likely to follow the curriculum of India Sunday School Union in the near future.

Leadership Training

Almost all the pastors in Zeliangrong Churches are laymen. The only primary means of the Bible Study and spiritual guidance for the pastors was the leadership training camp. Since there was no Bible School in the whole of Manipur before 1954, the missionary had to organise the Bible Camp every year in which the Bible Study, discussion, Church administration and simple preaching methods were taught. The training camp was one of the sources from which they learnt about God, Jesus Christ, the Bible and the Church.

Even now most of our Zeliangrong churches' pastors are untrained. They need to be given training. The Bible camp and training are the only places where they can learn about the ministry. Though some young graduates of the Bible school are beginning to serve in the churches it is not sufficient to meet the need of the Churches. Therefore, leadership training camp has been maintained as one of the projects in the Association by which pastors, evangelists and other church leaders are given the knowledge of Christ to run the church effectively.

Second World War and its Effects

The ascension of Bodhachandra Singh to the throne of Manipur in 1941 almost coincided with the coming of the Second World War to Asia, Since British justice previled everywhere there was no more danger of inter-tribal and village feuds. Everywhere there was deep peaceful atmosphere in the country. G. Even says. "In 1940 and 1941 the War had no direct impact on Manipur which still remains as one of the world's beautiful sports of peace."[1]

Imphal, the capital of Manipur, which had seemed so far removed from any possible battle began to feel the approaching of the war. In 1941 thousands of refugees from Burma began to pour into Imphal. A camp was established at Koirengei. And day and night the march went on. Many died on the road without food and shelter. Those who died were they fell; vultures were waiting above the refugees, camp. Everyday scores of the bodies were burnt. It was a horrible sight to see the refugees dying on the road. The sight of all these and the approaching news of terrible war threatened the lives of the people. Most of the hills' people believed that end of the world had come. They were expecting the immediate coming of Christ.

On May 10, 1942 the Japanese dropped bombs on Imphal killing many civilians and refugees. A second raid took place on May 16, 1942. Almost every house had been adandoned. The Christian Compound of Thngmeiband became a deserted place.[2]

By the end of 1943 the pang of the war was felt in the whole of Manipur. In 1945 the Japanese were badly defeated and were retreating into Burma. During the war many villages and churches were destroyed and vacated. The villagers fled to the jungles. Everything became costly and there was no food to buy and eat. In the midst of such calamities, the Christians' attitude was hopeful and quite different from that of the

1, C. Evans and James: Imphal (Macmillan & Co. Ltd. London 1962) p. 20.

2. For 13 years this plot of land could not be regained by the Christianr. Only in 1955 they got back. This place is the administrative centre for the Manipur Baptist Convention at present,

non-christians. T. Luikham says, "They were satisfied with the immediate results and took things as they came while the Christians gradually came to realise how the prophecies written in the Bible were being gradually fulfilled. Our faith increased and our belief in the Bible was more firmly established. Everywhere there was a possibility of religious persecution, but the Christians stood firm in their faith."[3]

After the war diseases visited the whole Manipur state and a great namber of lives were taken. On the other hand many modern scientific inventions such as aeroplane, bombs, guns and other weapons awakened and terrified the minds of the tribal people because they never knew about such things before. This contributed towards their minds accepting more of the civilised society.

The Zeliangrong Baptist Church at this time was active in spreading the Gospel. Mr. Laokeinang, Dinthuiyang, Tekhao and Matikbou were employed as evangelists. Mr. K. David, the son of Mr. Namrijinpou supervised the whole field as the first Superintendent pastor among the Zeliangrong Nagas When David was released from his Sub-pastorship, Mr. Keithonang, the first matriculate among the Zeliangrong replaced him. Unfortunately in the same year he passed away in the early winter 1942. As there was no able leader to take up this job, the post was left vacant for many years. The field work was carried out by the evangelist only. The Gospel of Christ, inspite of all difficulties, could reach even the remote area of the western side of the Barak river though the remnant of war and tragedy in the whole area was prevalent.

Organisation of the Church for her Mission

India achieved Independence in 1947. The spirit of freedom was soon prevalent everywhere in the country. The spirit of

3. T. Luikham : A short history of Manipur Baptist Christian Golden Jubilee Ukhrul, 1948, p. 30.

nationalism and tribalism became a stronghold of all the classes of the people. Nagas had very little or no contact with outsiders i.e. with the Hindu civilisation. With the coming of western civilisation, through the Baptist missionaries, Nagas were suddenly exposed to an entirely new culture, a new world had broken upon them. In addition to attainment of the freedom of India, great change had taken place. The love of freedom and the spirit of independence, in many cases, brought division and strife among the people.

The two tribes, the Zeliangrong Naga and the Kuki who were under one administration of North-west Area Association began to be conscious of their differences in culture and language. They began to sense their own needs. They wanted to have literature in their own languages. They began to feel that it would be better to divide the Association and let each manage their own Churches. At the same time they also understood that their missionaries would not be allowed to stay very long with them. They sensed that sooner or later the time would come when they ought to shoulder the responsibilities of the Church by themselves. The Kuki Christians had formed their own Association. The North-west Area Association continued to be run by the left-over combination of Hmar, Kom, Chiru, Liangmei, Zemei, Mpuimei and Rongmei Churches or groups when the Kukis separated in 1947.

In the same year the first Zeliangrong Conference of the inheritor of the North-west Association was held at Khongjaron and adopted the following resolutions that "The hereditable body will continue to serve the Lord with the help of the almighty hand of God. The main communicant language in the Association should be Rongmei.[4]"

The Zeliangrong Annual Association meeting was held in the following year at Vanchengphai village with total delegate

4. North-west Area Church Conference Action (Khongjaron 1947) Resolution No. 7.

of about one thousand. Mr. Mateibou and Mr. Ramjinang were commissioned to be the evangelists.

Later Missionaries

Rev. William Pettigrew left Manipur in 1933. Dr. Warlius took charge of the work of Manipur State with the help of Mr. Tanquist from Kohima, Naga Hills from 1934-1940. Dr. Alquist came to Manipur in 1940, with the help of Mr. Supplee from Kohima. He took the charge of the work of Manipur Christians. But unfortunately when Dr. Alquist was tranvelling between Kohima and Kangsokpi he was killed in a motor accident in 1941. Though his life was short he rendered a good service to those with defective sight. Being an eye specialist he was the only hope of the blind and many received their sight through his service.

After the death of Alquist, Rev Earl E. Brock came to Manipur in 1941 and served the Christians at the time of the invasion of Manipur by the Japanese in 1944. When he left Manipur, Mr. John S. Anderson came to Manipur in 1946. Mr. Anderson carried out a valuable service for Zeliangrong Christians. He published a Rongmei hymn book and sent Mr. Namthiurei and Mr. Jikamang to Jorhat Bible School in 1950. Unfortunately Mr. Jikamang passed away during his Bible Study period. Mr. Namthiurei was the first Bible Graduate among the Zeliangrong Nagas. And he was the first Executive Secretary of the North-west Area Association. He also took up as part time worker in translating the Rongmei Bible. During this time he compiled Rongmei Church Hymnal and chorus booklet. He served as field director of the Association after Mr. Meingan for five years term (1969-1974).

Rev. John S. Anderson was the last missionary in Manipur. The Naga Independent movement was rising in the whole Naga areas in Naga Hills and Manipur. At the same the Manipur Government, particularly Meitei Hindus were against the Missionary very much from preaching the words of the Gospel.

Thus, Rev. Anderson was finally ordered to leave Manipur never to return and he moved to Jorhat, Assam on the 8th November 1954.

These were the words of the last missionary in Manipur: "Quite naturally, perhaps, the ministry of Christ in Manipur by all possible means shall continue to be our interest and prayers for a long time time to come, even though we shall no longer have opportunity to be a part of that ministry. May God grant to our beloved brethren there the wisdom and the power to carry on."[5]

Though the missionary left Manipur, the Churches of the Zeliangrongs were not affected. Since the missionary era of the long thirty years, the Zeliangrong people and the churches were carrying on their ministry all alone. They did not receive assistance and help from them. whereas the Tangkhuls and Kukis were given Bible and hymn book with many other assistance in the field of education by the missionaries. Before the Second World War 1944, there were many matriculates and graduates among the Tangkhuls and Kukis whereas among the Zeliangrong Nagas the light of education started only after the war, Therefore the Zeliangrong Church and its people were more than thirty years behind other tribes. Zeliangrong church were self-propagating and self-governing from its inception. They are self-struggling people.

5. CBCAM : Report of Assam Mission : Council of Baptist Churches in Assam and Manipur, Gauhati, 1954-55, p. 67.

CHAPTER IV

Development of the Propagation of the Gospel

Organisations

Establishment of the Christian Centre

The North-west Association was supervised from Kangpokpi with great difficulty. After the secession of the Kukis the Zeliangrong people began to think of establishing a Centre of their own. The villagers of the Tamenglong Village and Khongjaron village offered their lands for the purpose. After praying seeking the guidance of the Lord, the choice went for Kongjaron where the mission centre was subsequently opened in 1949.

In the same year evangelist Mr. Dinthuiyang was appointed to the post of the Superintending Pastor which had been vacant for the previous six years after the death of Mr. Keithonang. Mr. Dinthuiyang was asked to come over to the newly selected mission location. Thus he and his family moved to the Centre, cleared the jungle, and built a temporary thatch house. After a year Mr. Ramon was appointed as evangelist and he was asked to come to the Centre and accordingly he moved there to take up the new challange. The Zeliangrong Association was grateful the Khongjaron Village for their generous offering of land for the use of its mission work.

The Association had been looking for some dedicated trained young men who could take up the mission work of the Association. God answered the prayers by sending a faithful young man by name of Mr. Meingan Panmei, a graduate of Eastern Theological College, Jorhat, Assam, to be the first Field Director of the Association. He assumed his Field Directorship in December 1956. There after, the real developmental work of the mission began. A few houses were constructed and new projects were planned out. A Bible School building, Hostel, the Association Office, the Bible Translation office, a chapel building and youth and women offices were built. The library was also opened in the Mission Centre. The Zeliangrong Association was revived with a new spirit and interest in the work of the mission. They were active in preaching the Word of God. In this year a new Church was organised at Magulong. The number of Christians had doubled. The baptised membership was reported to be 5760 at the end of the year 1956. The Christian Churches were planted throughout Manipur as the Gospel of Christ spread like wild fire. The Missionaries had organised all the different tribal groups to come together as the great need was felt for unity in the love of Christ. Thus the Manipur Baptist Convention was organised and formed in the loose fellowship type. The first convention was held at Kangpokpi in 1928 and more than 1100 Christians from ten Tribal groups gathered together for fellowship and inspiration. The second convention meeting was held at Ismael (now shifted to Sirarakhong) in 1931. And the third at Imphal in 1934. Thus all the Associations of the different tribes were pulled together in the MBC. The North-west Area Association known as Manipur Baptist Association No. IV was officially affiliated to the MBC and the recogniation was given officially by the Council of Baptist Churches in North-East India (CBCNEI) in 1955.

The name Manipur Baptist Association No. IV was changed to Zeliangrong Baptist Association in 1977 when the numbering system was dropped officially by MBC and CBCNEI because the awareness and identification of its own Tribal name for recognition was a satisfactory answer in the movement of Tribal Society. The ZBA Centre at Khongjaron has been a common activity centre of the Church for the whole Zeliangrong Nagas. The Zeliangrong has four different speaking dialects. So for convenience of the spreading of the Gospel, the Association was divided into four fellowships such as Zemei, Liangmei, Rongmei and Puimei. Subsequently the fellowships were turned into full-fledged Associations as Zemei Naga Baptis-Association, Liangmei Naga Baptist Association, Rongmei Naga Baptist Associaion and puimei Naga Baptist Association. The recognition was given officially by the MBC in 1987. However, the Zeliangrongs were never divided. The Zeliangrong Baptist Churches Council (ZBCC) was formed as their common platfrom and administrative centre was still Khongjaron Christian Centre. Rev. Kaiba Riamei, M. Div. is the Executive Secretary of ZBCC.

The following sub-centre have established for following four dialective group of the Reliangrong Baptist Associations in in Manipur State :

(a) Rongmei Naga Baptist Association at Tamenlgong Head Quarters;

(b) Liangmei Naga Baptist Association at Tamei Head Quaters;

(c) Zemei Naga Baptist Association at Taosem Head Quarters;

(d) Puimei Naga Baptist Association at Haochong Head Quarters.

As stated before, the Zeliangrong Nagas live in compact area covering Nagaland, Manipur and Assam in North Cachar Hills. In Nagaland, the Centre for the Zemei Baptist Association is at Peren, for the Liangmei at Taning and for Rongmei at Zaluk (Kabeikamning).

Due to the political division, the Zeliangrong people were distributed and divided in their integrity and unity. They have been forced to become neglected and secluded from each other. It was made difficult to keep in contact among themselves. As the reason four dialect such as Rongmei, Liangmei Zemei and Puimei have been spoken by Seliangrong. Even among the Zemei of the Southern section of Nagaland and North Cachar Hills, Haflong covering 120 villages speak one dialeat and the northern Zemeis in Nagaland covering only about 40 villages speak different dialects, Therefore they are facing problems in printing the Bible and other literature. In regard to Rongmei and Liangmei there is no problem; they speak the same language whether they belong to one State or the other in North-east. The Zemeis in the North Cachar Hills are Presbyterians. The Welsh Presbyterian Missionaries came first and worked among them. The missionaries allowed them to drink the local rice bear. Thus the drinking habit among the Zemei Presbyterians was never given up. The missinon's vision was altogether lost. The spiritual life was cooled down and there was no growth of the Church for the last many years. The Revival broke out among the Zeliangrang in Manipur and Nagaland in 1978. The burden for bringing the Gospel of Christ to his fellow brethren among the Zemei in Haflong area have been aroused. The Holy Spirit directly called the people to go to N.C. Hills and proclaim the love gospel of Jesus. As led by the Holy Spirit batch after batch from many churches went and witnessed about Christ and thus many people came forward to accept the Gospel. Many people confessed and repened of their sins and accepted the Lord Jesus Christ and thus many Churches have been planted. The number of the Baptist Churches so far planted were more than 17.

The Zeliangrong in N.C. Hills were pre-dominantly the believers of the Haraka religion which has been founded by Haipou Jadonang and Rani Gaidinliu in about 1930 during the Zeliangrong Rebellion. Till today the Haraka believers are the majority in almost every village. The need of preaching and bringing the Gospel of Jesus Christ among the Zeliangrongs in Haflong (N.C. Hills) is very acute and urgent.

The strong need for coming together was felt by the Zeliangrong Church Leaders in North East India and do the common cause of the Gospel of Jesus-Christ. Thus they organised a Zeliangrong Baptist Church Leaders Fellowship in 1981 at Tarung Baptist Church Imphal Valley in Manipur. Mr. Bikau Pamei and Mr. Timothy Phaomei were the first honorary President and Secretary respectively. The first Fellowship meeting was held at New Jaluke Baptist Church, Nagaland in 1983; the second at Zeliangrong Baptist Church, Dimapur, Nagaland; the third at Tamenglong Baptist Church in 1985; the fourth was held at Rongmei Baptist Church at Kohima and the fifth meeting was held Tamei in 1987. After a series of discussion and consultation the Baptist Union of Zeliongrong (BUZ) was formed and its constitution was drafted which was to be studied and approved by the Zeliangrong Churches. However, due to change of leadership, lack of good leadership and co-ordination of the whole Zeliangrong Churches in North-east and implementation for fuller organisation of BUZ could not be materialised properly yet. It is the belief and hope that this needful and cherished expectation will come around for serving the Lord together as one Zeliangrong unit.

The disintegrity and the political division has been made by the British Colonial Imperialism. Therefore, the national Government of India was not to be blamed. However, if the Government of India at present is for rescuing the human right and safeguard the integrity of the people concerned, something must be done. Now the Zeliangrong Nagas are minority in each State and therefore, their privileges in the society and political welfare are denied or is minimum. The development programme in each three States were overlooked by the Government. The people have not been provided even their basic needs of water supply, electricity road and communication. They have been neglected for too long. For this reason the

Zeliangrong people were very much behind other fellow Tribal groups in the North-east. However, the Zeliangrong Christians were depending on themselves self propagating, self support and self government. The good Lord in His grace and mercy has given them His blessings that steadily they grew and expanded His Kingdom. The following are the statistics record of the Zeliangrong Baptist Christians in North-east India:

States	*No. of Churches*	*No. of Baptised Members*	*Total No. of Christian*
In Manipur			
Rongmai Naga	130	10,162	45,260
Liangmei Naga	47	6,359	19,077
Zemei Naga	31	1,758	3,274
Puimei	11	1,066	1,198
In Nagaland			
Zemei Naga	54	5,801	35,000
Liangmei Naga	13	1,500	4,500
Rongmei Naga	9	1,012	3,036
In Assam			
Rongmei Naga	40	872	2,616
Zemei Naga	13	210	630

Bible School

The North-West Association was growing rapidly as the people took the responsibility of making known the revelation of God in Jesus Christ of many. As the Churches has been expanding many new programmes were undertaken, but something more had to be ventured. The leaders of the Association sensed the pulse of the people and also were convinced that the

Lord was with them. They realised their weakness in attempting to be shepehereds of the Lord's people because of their lack of knowledge of Biblical doctrine. They felt the need to train young men and women to be ministers in the Churches.

With the help of the Council of Baptist Churches in North-East India (CBCNEI) they opened a Bible School at the Christian Centre in 1959. In the beginning the school had 18 boys and 2 girls enrolled. Mr. K. G. Simon and Mr. M.P. Namthiurei graduates of Eastern Theological College, came to teach in the school. God blessed the school and as it grew it served the Churches very profitably.

The Bible schools has two training programmes: the three year course, known as Diploma course and an in-service training course for lay pastors and leaders of the Churches that lasts one year. Now about one hundred graduates of this school are serving in the Association as pastors, evangelists, youth and women's leaders and Sunday school teachers. Through establishment of the Bible school, the Churches have grown stronger and have been able to stand on their own feet with these trained leaders. Establishment of the Centre and the Bible school meant the Churches shared more of the responsibility in the service of the Lord's mission.

Youth Fellowship

In the early stage of the Church of Zeliangrong Naga, Youth organizations were not encouraged by the Association. This may have been because the Morung[1] system for young people, which was the basic social life of Nagas in the non-Christian villages, was denied and prohibited by the early missionaries for the Christians. The Morung was regarded as a heathen practice. During this transitional period from Morung system to

1. Morung is a youth club. It has separate houses for boys and girls. They come to their morung and sleep. They learn their cultural customary and social life from the Morung in the village.

Christian-Youth-formed organization, the church simply could not provide activities for Christian young people in a Christian context.

As the Church grew, they felt a special concern for the young people. When the North-West Area Association conen-tion was held in 1939 at Taobam village, the conference unanimously agreed to organise a Christian Endeavour Society in each local Church. However the early society did not func-tion properly as there was no one trained to guide them. In 1950 youth leaders began to from a union under the instruction of Mr. Kiulingpou of Tamenglong Bapt. Courch. The Christian Endeavour was reformed in the pattern of 'Christian Endeavour Four Square' by V.W. Abbey. Mr. Kiusenang of Tamenglong Church was appointed as the first president of C.E. Union. The C.E. organization performed preaching groups an social camps. From time to time they visited different Churches, as well as non-Christian villages, preaching, teaching, singing and encouraging the people to dedicate their lives to Christ. Through these youth activities the Churches were grealty strengthened.

In 1947 Rev. R.G. Beers came as a youth missionary to CBCNEI. He gave special training in Baptist youth Fellowship organization. Thus in most of the CBCNEI Churches BYF organization was introduced. The Zeliangrong Association also adopted BYF Union in 1962. Mr. I.D. Thuanbui was appointed the C.E. Union President in 1957 and in 1962 that was change to youth Director according to CBCNEI youth organiation.

BYFU office was maintained at the Church at Khongjaron with three full time workers, a Director and Youth promoters. Every Saturday a young peoples' programme was held in each local Church in the whole Association.

Women's Socicty

The Zeliangrong Naga women possess strong character. They are actively involved in the work of the Church. In the social structure of the Church, they have equal status with men. In every local Church the women from their own organization and they help the Church through these organizations.

Every cooking-time each women keeps aside a handful of rice which is put together in a fund used for the work the Chureh. They also bring vegetables, which they grow in their gardens and farms and fire-wood to the worship service every Sunday as part of their offering to the Lord. Later they sell them at market rate. A large part of the Church's income thus comes from the women's society.

The women society in the Association has been doing a tremendous job in the proclamation of the word of God. Since 1949 they sent an evangelist by name Ramjinang to preach the Gospel among the non-Christians.

As present the women society employs three full time workers. The President, who is in charge of the office, and two evangelists. They are constantly travelling to different Churches giving spiritual guidance to women and preaching the Gospel to those who have not heard about Christ.

Division of Circles in the Association

In order to carry out the mission work quickly and effectively, the Association was put in order into four Circles. From each circle a person was appointed to represent in the Association Executive Committee which was called the working Committee. This Committee was responsible for the vorious projects of the Association such as evangelistic work, Sunday schools and mission schools. In Longdi Conference in 1949 the following persons were elected in the Committee: Mr. Namsadai for South Circle, Mr. Miklao for North Circles, Mr. Rommon for the West Circle and Mr. Gaikhuijei for the Centre Circle. This Committee heartily served the Association for more than ten years.

The Association realised that the circle organization was very valuable and effective in building the Association. Therefore, they appointed full time evangelists in each circle. The evangelists had the responsibility for bringing the word of God to their circles. In each circle one part-time secretary was also employed. The Centres for each circle have been opened and the secretariat handled the office work of the circles. The centres for the circle are as follow: Saramba Centre for the West circle, Rongdai for the Centre Circle, Langmei for North circle and None (Longmai) for South circle. The evangelists and the secretaries now reside in their respective centres.

Self-Support and Self-Propagation

The question of self-support is the current problem of the Indian Church. In one Association meeting, Rev. B. I. Anderson, a missionary to North-east India spoke on the subject of self-support saying, "Young birds want to stay always in the nest expecting food from the mother. But when the mother knows that it is time for the young ones to leave the nest, she will push them out knowing the ability of the young ones to fly and search for food for themselves".[2] The Zeliangrong Churches from the beginning managed themselves under their indigenous leadership. They supported their own institutions, Pastors and evangelists. The converts were taught to exercies their Christian stewardship as an outward expression of their inner change of hearts.

Most of the people of this area were cultivators and had very little money. There were some tithers among the teachers, but little money was collected otherwise. Most of the funds were raised by the sale of domestic animals, vegetables and rice brought as offerings. The major income of the Church came from paddy which was sold. The money from the sale was used for the work of the Church.

2. CNBNEI : Baptist work in Nortn East India (Cauhati 1961) p. 47.

In the early years the Zeliangrong Christians undertook the entire support of the preacher at a salary of five rupees a month. Sometime the villagers had to go and cultivate the field of the pastor as a payment of his salary. This became the practice because the ideal of independence in the local support of pastor was taught.

Prior to 1933 Evangelists were employed throught the Missionary fund of Kangpokpi. But the mission support was discontinued from 1933 and two evangelists were employed with only eight rupees per month as salary.[3] Without proper payment they laboured freely in the service of the King.

With the beginning of the Indian Independence the Christians came to the sudden relization that a new world had broken upon them. They greeted this new world with mixed feelings of joy, fear and suspicion. They began to understand that their missionaries would not be with them permanently. The reflection on this situation awakened the Church to a new sense of selfhood. As a result the chunch began to belong to the local people. This caused the Church to become quite dynamic and forward looking.

The local pastors and the evangelists of the Zeliangrong Nagas are still laymen, without Bible School or Seminary training, yet many of them are genuine Christians and no one can question their faith and integrity. The Church has been growing steadily under their indigenous leadership. The Church is self-governing and self-supporting with an evangelistic mission of its own. Though the missionaries left suddenly from Manipur, the Zeliangrong Churches were not affected greatly. At present the Association employs 18 workers of which four are BYF workers and three are women's workers.

The Association launched an outreach project which consisted of two or three evangelists who were sent to proclaim the

3. MP. Namthiurei : The Great Awakening : (Golden Jublee publication, Tamenglong, Manipur, 1972) p. *18*.

love story of Jesus Christ to the areas untouched or unreached by the Gospel. Though they were employed on a part time basis, a tremendous work could be carried out in addition to the regular work of the Association. As there so many people yet unreached by the message of Christ, the Association began placing more emphasis on evangelistic work. It has beed an activity of the whole Church which believes that everything has to be originated from within so that the Chrch can be totally self-supporting.

Literature

The Zeliangrong Nagas were once out of civilization. They had no written literature of their own, but they maintained strange legendary notion. Their believed that long long ago they had a written language. Their stories were recorded. It was written on the dry skin of animals. The plain people also had the same record written on leaves. These records were handed down by God to them. The Nagas could not keep it it any longer as it was animal skin and they ate it up, but the plain people kept it carefully. Therefore, the plain people have their own Scripts and literatures today.

Among the Zeliangrong Nagas a legend is told that there was a man named Amung who built a Magnificient House. He arranged a big feast for the whole earth. This was called "Amung kai zoulumei". All human kind from the four corners of the earth came together for feasting, drinking and dancing. All kinds of living creatures were also gathered and they were given their respective names. The written scripts and record was given to human kind. According to that record on that day the creation of all things and living beings on the earth had taken place. A written record was also given to mankind. However, where it is now, nobady knows. It had disappeared.

In the time of Jadonang's movement in 1927, the ancient Naga scripts were said to have been found once again by the prophet Jadonang. He introduced them and taught his followers how to read and write. The hymns were written in that script. It was also said that Jadonang wrote a petition to the British Sub-Divisional Officer of Tamenglong in that script. The officer summoned Jadonang to his office and asked him to read the petition for him. Jadonang kept silent. Out of anger the office burnt the petition. At present it is not possible to find out where the script is. The army destroyed all the properties of Jadonang. His disciples who know the scripts are no more in existence.

There are some among the Zeliangrong educated people undertaking a research of the script, A man named Mr. Laokeinang of Longrang who has much interest in this research work, found the script. He believed that it was the ancient Nagas' script which were lost in antiquity. He handed over these scripts to me. They are readable and usable. Below are the letters ane the sound they represent :

Letters

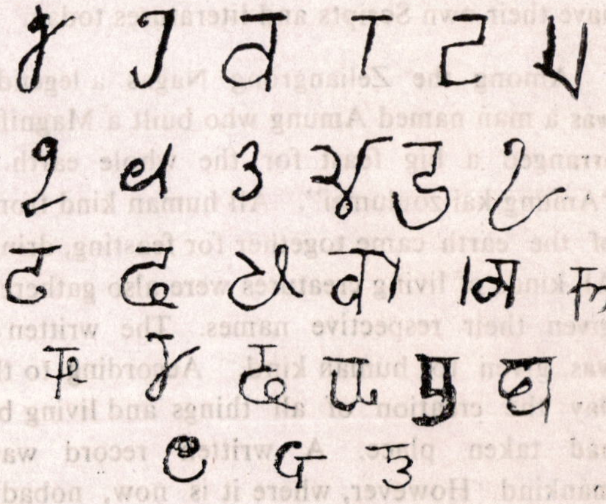

Sounds a-wa a-oi ni-i ni-e E E-ui E-ya n hu gou ngou dou Thya tu taphi mi nu lai pu bei awo chich kiya rou ash zei

Numerical

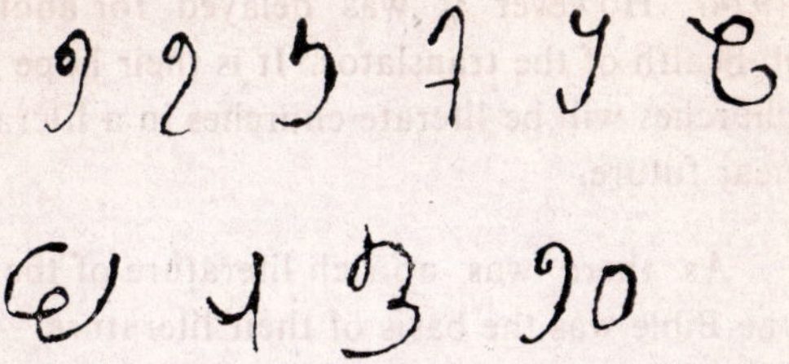

Sooner or later the Church of the Nagas became interested in having their own scripts adopted. It is the sincere belief of the author that if the State Government as well as the Central Government would take interest and encourage them to continue their work, the future Nagas will have a written language and literature.

The tribal language in North-East India developed when the Missionaries introduced the Roman Script. The use of Roman Script is so rooted that it will take time to introduce a new script among the Naga and yet it depends on the interest and acceptance of the people. If we are to develop the Naga culture and tradition they must use written language and literature that fit their own spoken language.

Among the Zeliangrong Nagas Mr. K. David was the first patron of literature. He prepared and published the first Rongmei Primer which had been used in the schools for many years. He contributed his skill and talent to bring the light of literature among the Rongmei speaking people. At present the Association has organised the Literature Committee. Through this Committee a lot of literature has been produced for school text books.

Bible Translation Works

The Bible Society of India is helping the Zeliangrong Christians in translating the Bible. For more than fifteen years they were Christians without the Bible in their own language. The people were happy and rejoiced with the hope that the New

Testament in Rongmei Naga will be available by the end of 1974. However it was delayed for another five years due to ill health of the translator. It is their hope that the Zeliangrong churches will be literate churches in a literate community in the near future.

As there was no rich literature of the Zeliangrong Nagas, the Bible was the basis of their literature. As for the Rongmei Naga, the complete Bible translation has been done. They were very much grateful to the Bible Society of India for their kind assistance in employing Rev. Gaikhuanlung Gangmei to be the translator. The Bible is scheduled for distribution in August, 1989. The Liangmei and Zemei translation was also in progress. As for the last so many years they had no usable standard hyman book to be used in the Church worships. Now for the Rongmei Nagas a "Himdai Lu" has been compiled containing 500 selected gospel hymns, expecting to be released along with the Rongmei Bible.

The Bible and the hymns always go together. They are the words of God which are the means of instruction and teaching the people. They are the basis for upliftment and growth of literacy of one language in communication to man and God. The best literature we ever find is in the language of the Bible and hymn.

For many years without the Bible and hymn book, the Zeliangrong Christians went on. They were given Manipuri Bible which they could not read properly and understand. Misinterpretation of the language and funny reading were their problem in the worship services in the Church. Since 1942, the demand for translation of the Bible was placed, however, uptill 1952 the work could not be completed. When M.P. Namthiurei, a graduate of the Jorhat Bible School, took up the translation work with the assistance of Mr. K.G. Simon and Miss J.A. Rose from Cachar, Assam. First they published the Gospel of Luke and John in 1960.

When Mr. K.G. Simon went for his theological studies at Jorhat, Mr. Namthiurei again continued his translation work at Tamenglong and completed the book of Acts and Romans and were ready for publication. And the Scripture Gift Mission and the CBCNEI helped in publishing several scripture booklets such as Lost and Found, the Good Shepherd and the story of Jesus in Rongmei Naga. The CBCNEI also helped towards the Bible translation project. By the time when Mr. K.G. Simon completed his seminary studies, he was employed as a part-time Bible translator. The increasing demand for having Bible in their language was so much pressurised that Simon was released from the Principalship of the Bible School, at Khongjaron and entered into the full time Bible translation work in 1964. Immediately the Bible Society of India paid his salary. Thus among the Zeliangrong Nagas, the Rongmei New Testament was first published and came out in 1979, the Liangmei Naga New Testment came out in 1983 and Zemei's in 1984. At present Mr. N.K. Shing is working on Liangmei Naga and Mr. Heutui and Rev. Kuame on Zemei. It is expected that the Zeliangrong Church will have the whole Bible without much delay.

CHAPTER V

The Contemporary Situation

Formation of the Zeliangrong Union

We are living in the modern world in which everything is on the move. With the discovery of the electricity, Radio, T.V., penicillin and food preservation, large scale of the Space age automic and nuclear power, technology of the twentieth century, and all advancement in science, theology is taking a new turn. The miraculous divine creation, formally seen by primitive man in every breeze, in thunder, lightning, in the return of the Spring and Summer, does not have meaning any longer. The Science has, to a large extent, taken away the miraculous vision in nature, which once produced awe, and wonder for the divine. The new everything is natural. So the radical theologians tell us that God is dead. They challenge man to stand on his feet and prove to himself as 'man come of age'.

This emerging situation of a revolutionary age causes effects an all human situations—religious, political and social. This new decade says that the Church has a greater task than before. This situation arund us demands that we should act and act quickly if we are to exercise our double stewardship to be faithful and enterprising in our own sphere of secular life and duties and help others to be so. The Church can held best by encouraging the development of knowledge and ability, and by redeeming men's will and motives from whatever is evil in them.

In dealing with this new situation and problem one must not forget to look back to the past, learn from the present, and decide for the future. Therefore let us examine some of the aspects of the Zeliangrong Nagas' Movement in recent years. For the last many years since the time of British Rule in India the Zeliangrong Nagas has been deprived of their rightful claim. The Zeliangrong Rebellion of Haipou Zadonang and Rani Gaidinliu against the regime of Manipur Maharaja and the British Colonialism was the mark of their cry for their political unity.

Right after India's Independence, the Zeliangrong Leaders from Manipur, Nagaland and Assam came together and formed a political union called "Eliangrong Union" at Keishamthong Village, Imphal, in 1948. This Union has been functioning and repeatedly demanding the Indian Union, submitting several memorand a for their special development work and unity. However nothing was heard whatsoever for the last forty years and more. There were practical difficulties on the part of the Government of India though Pandit Nehru, the first Prime Minister and Shrimati Indira Gandhi had real sympathy for the cause of the Zeliangrong people. Because Zeliangrong were divided politically and distributed in three states of North-east India, to do development work in a special category was difficult and to meet their demand has to be referred to the concerned state governments and thus there had been a lot of bias in the real implementations. A past form pinodic talks the demands are kept pending, ignoring and forgetting the genuine claim and demand of the Zeliangrongs.

Now the Zeliangrong Nagas in the North-East were alerted and they have started reviving their rightful and genuine deman for complete unity and integrity of all the Zeliangrong

Nagas in the North-East India. 'The Zeliangrong People Convention' was formed and they had submitted a memorandum and made several trips sending their delegation to meet and interview with Rajiv Gandhi' the Prime Minister and the Central Authorities in New Delhi several times. The Central Government is reconsidering and giving attention to the cause of the Zeliangrong Nagas. The late Prime Minister Indira Gandhi remarked and said in response to their demand to Rani Gaidinliu, the President of the Zeliangrong People Convention.

> "Let me assure you that the welfare of the Zeliangrong people will always receive my greatest sympathy and prompt consideration."

A consistent note of demand for Zeliangrong Homeland is quoted here below :

Rani Gaidinliu, President of Zeliangrong People Convention sumbitted a memorandum in New Delhi in 1986 to the Prime Minister of India. As a follow-up action of their demand the ZPC had also launched several bandhs and hartals in all Zeliangrong inhabited areas in North-east. The following are reproduction from the memorandum :

Demand for Zeliangrong Homeland

The Zeliangrong People's Convention made a Declaration for a Zeliangrong Homeland in November 1982 and sumitted a memorandum on the Zeliangrong Homeland within the Indian Union in Oct. 1983. It is the unanimous demand of the Zeliangrong people that the Zeliangrong areas now scattered in the three states of Assam, Manipur and Nagaland are to be integrated into a common homeland. The ZPC had two rounds of talk with the Prime Minister like Indiraji on this issue.

1. Rani Gaidinliu : Memorandum submitted to Honorable Shri Rajiv Gandhi, Prime Minister of India, 1986.

Now the Zeliangrong People's Convention reintegrates the demand for Zeliangrong Homeland. The followitg points are being restated and quoted :

1. The Zeliangrong people are occupying a compact and contiguous area over the Barail Mountain Ranges over the area of Assam, Nagaland and Manipur. The ZPC asserts the historical prerogative over this territory for the formation of a state within the Indian Union.
2. The Zeliangrong people under the leadership of Haipou Jadonang and Rani Gaidinliu fought against the British and suffered under the oppressive rule of the Colonial power. The Zeliangrong people hope of being provided the opportunity to live under a single political and administrative roof has been redeemed in free India.
3. The Zeliangrong people want to integrate all the Zeliangrong inhabited areas of Assam, Nagaland and Manipur into a separate state within the Indian Union.
4. The ZPC will use peaceful, democratic and constitutional means for the fulfilment of its political objective.
5. The ZPC stands for unity and integrity of India. Now the ZPC solemnly urges the Government of India to seriously consider this rightful demand of the Zeliangrong people in view of the contiuning insurgency of the extremist elements in lhe Zeliangrong areas.

On Economic Development

In course of our discussion with the late Prime Minister Indiraji and other Central leaders, we were told that economic development would be provided to Zeliangrong areas of the three states-Assam, Nagaland and Manipur. The Planning Commission and NEC formed a fact-finding committee to examine the problem. (Planning Commission letter No. 16/38/84 NEI d. 11/2/1985 copy enclosed). But so far no specific programme has been spelt out either by the Centre or NEC or the state Governments. While the stand that unless a separate state is created, no real economic development can be brought about, remains unchanged, we submit the following proposal for the examination by the Central Government.

1. The creation of a statutory Central Development of the Zeliangrong areas of North-East India.
2. The protection of Zeliangrong People's customary and traditional rights over land and forest. No land and forest laws either of the Centre or the states should be introduced against the consent of the people.
3. The establishment of the statutory of Zeliangrong Council to deal with the tribal customary laws and cultural affairs.
4. The traditional village council should be given a statutory status as an administrative unit, a court of law and an agency of development.
5. Establishment of Zeliangrong Rifles, a para military force for the Zeliangrong Areas. It should be established by the Central Government of India.
6. A University College under a Central University and a central agricultural university should be established in Zeliangrong areas.

I urge you to consider our demand with sympathy and with a sense of urgency. Our poverty, our hunger, our ignorance, our diseases and our general backwardness can not be eradicated unless our political and economic demands are fulfilled. Lastly, I believe in the peaceful solution of our problem. I hope and trust that a meaningful dialogue between the Government and the ZPC will follow out of this submission.

With the highest regards and deep affection, may the Almighty grant you the wisdom, courage and strength to lead our great nation to great height of glory. It is our confidence that just like you solved the Punjab tangle and the foreigner issue in Assam and the Mizo people keeping the national interests well protected, you will surely concede our demand. It is my sincere and cherished wish that in the evening of my life, my life-long dream of uniting my Zeliangrong people will be achieved with your help."[2]

Zeliangrong Ringtelau !!

Some of the Characteristics of Zeliangrong Nagas

These are some of the characteristics in the early time and to see how far they can be-examined and renewed in the light of changing situation of the present days.

The Zeliangrong Nagas developed some special characteristics peculiar to them. Although a great danger in hasty generalisation, which cannot be completely avoided in such an attempt at self-study, we have to consider a few of our obvious characteristics.

1. We have already noticed in the first chapter that Zeliangrongs have deep love for the land in which they live and their loyalty to all those who live in it. The tribe is knitted together as a large family.
2. They had no one to approach for help in their day to day work of food gathering and self preservation against enemies of various kinds. This taught them self-reliance. One of the manifestations of this self-reliance can be seen in the way the Churches support themselves.
3. The self-reliance pre-supposes hard work and they find that they are industrious like pigeons. The parent-pigeon industriously brings grain of corn to its young ones and flies off once again immediately in search of another without losing any time. The Zeliangrongs keep busy throughtout their lives for their livelihood.

2. Rani Gaidinliu : Memorandum Submitted to Honorable Shri Rajiv Gandhi, Prime Minister, New Delhi, 1986.

4. Zeliangrong Nagas are conservative in out-look. They do not like to change their old ways. They like to live as they have lived for ages. The new methods of agriculture, craftsmanship, medical treatment and education, for example, do not immeditaely appeal to them. When the youngor generation land themselves readily to new fashions they fear that their old ways of living may be destroyed. The conservatism expresses itself in a passion for relating Christianity to their indigenous ancient culture and for bringing all the good things from that culture into the Church.

5. Zeliangrong Nagas value truthfulness, honesty, sincerity and guiltlessness. V. Elwin says, "The Kabuis (Zeliangrongs) of Eastern (sic) Manipur are among the most attractive tribal people in India. Graceful, hospitable and industrious, they combined delicate sensitivity with an impeccable taste for design and colours."[3] We have to confess however, that we are losing some of these good qualities in the changing circumstances of the present days.

6. Though the Zeliangrong people can show remarkable courage and fortitude, they are timid and shy before other human beings. Fear has been a great handicap for them. Parents are too much in the habit of quieting crying babies by threatening them with evil spirits and so the children tend to develop fears.

7. One evil which has been their curse for ages is excessive use of intoxicating liquors. Two main drinks are very common rice beer and potent spirit distilled from the rice called 'Zouzu'. The rice beer is occassionally used for religious purposes. They are suffering from numerous evil consequences of excessive drinking. Refrom in

3. V. Elwin : The Tribal World : (Oxford University Press 1964) p. 228. The Zeliangrongs are living mostly in the western Hills of Manipur.

this regard is vital and is a challenge for almost all the people. Drug meance young the from people is past increasing which spoil the bright future among the Zeliangrongs. Precemtion, teaching and a education should be done of quickly.

Adoption of Christian Teachings

Christ's teaching spread rapidly among the Zeliangrong Nagas. Now 50% of the people are followers of Christ. They live in the villages. The villages are on the top of the high mountains. An averagevillage consists of fifty to three hundred families and every man and woman is praising the Lord from the top of the mountain. Thank the Lord, for God uses these people for His glory.

When Christ's message gets across into their hearts, their faith in Christ becomes so strong and yet their faith is very simple. They find their faith alive in the living personal God. God has become real to their daily practical lives. Jesus Christ was a new revelation to them. They are simple and honest and they believe everything which has been told in the Bible.

Secondly, they also feel a sense of self-sacrifice and dedication. They are so enthusiastic about the Gospel that they are ready to give everything they have for the sake of Christ. One volunteer evangelist on one occassion said, "I am happy to render my service in preaching the Gospel to people freely. If I were employed as pay-worker, I will have no reward in Heaven". This same spirit of self-sacrifice was prevalent among the early Christians.

Thirdly, the Christian unity was also achieved on account of deep sense of the brotherhood of men in the Lord Jesus. The bitterness between tribes and between villages had completely vanished. This resulted in unspeakable joy and happiness With this strong sense of Christian unity, regardless of tribes, languages and cultures, they mixed freely and accepted one another as brothers in Christ.

We have mentioned earlier that the achievement of India's Independence and modernisation in the 20th century brought an entirely new situation among the people. Pride in their own culture and tradition, communalism and tribalism, and nationalim became so strong that the life of the Church, to some extent, had been affected. These problems and divisions very among ourselves today. The older Christians of today remember the' good old days' in comparision to the present, which according to them is full of dissension, hatred and dlvision. For example, the Kuki and Naga Churches differ to those which existed befor the Independence.

The good qualities of Christianity such as unity, peace, and job in the Churches seem to be disappearing among them. We find the Christians who profess to be Christian on the outside are not Christians in reality. The present Christian attitude to mission and the work of the Church is insufficiently built upon Christian practice and belief. The Church of today has greater responsibility to deal with the young generation with a new vision and programme.

Impact of Modern Secular Trends on the Church

Through the centuries the Church has proclaimed her Lord Jesus Christ as the hope of the world. But now the world is proclaiming another voice the so called 20th century sceular man's voice. This voice proclaims that the hope of the world lies in scientific and technological advancement. This procees of secularisation in which men is placed free for religious utterancy results in the worship of the Church, her activities, her literatures, her budget seeming irrelevant to equip the people for life in the world.

The Church was also affected by the uprising of communalism which threatens to destroy secular democracy. Clashes occurred between Nagas and Kukis, with dissension between hills and plains, and the demand of merger of the Nagas of Manipur to Nagaland State, the Zeliangrong People's Convention movement demanding for separation etc. This communalism became the chief motivating force in the major crises. The secular character of the State in this very special sense has become the test of our democracy, because communalism would compel us along the paths of fascism.

Uprising of secular character also collapses moral values. We witnessed the absence of honest dealing in all matters; drinking and sexual immorality have increased. Bribery in the administrative machinery has become very ramphant.

The Church today is really facing the acute problem of the modern secular trends. We need to understand that the Church and its Gospel is related to the world and its affairs. Secular and secularism have varient meanings but when we speak of secular we think of the freedom, power and responsibility that God has given to men to order his own life and afiairs in the world. The secular world is God's world into which Christ came to save. The Church is committed to its stewardship. If the Church refuses to accept this responsibility, she is rejecting the full call of God.

The time has come to rethink and re-examine the programme and the activities of the Zeliangrong's Association with an understanding of the rapid moving situation in secular modren world so as to present the position and stand of the Church as relevant to its envirnment.

Effect of Education on Christian Youth

Illiteracy and ignorance have been characteristic of Zeliangrong Nagas. But today education is one of the most potent factors briniging about change in their lives. It is also a creed of the Government of India that all citizens should be made literate in the shortest possible time. To achieve this end special provisions have been made for the ribal people to bring them up to the level equal to the rest of the advanced communities. Thus many of the church's schools have been converted into government schools. A lot of money began to pour in towards the development—giving scholarships, for constructing roads and for the improvement of the tribal culture. The reaction to these immediate plans in Tribal Areas created a kind of confusion as to how to use their money in a proper way. They were at the loss as to how to accept the development work and programme offered to them. The young people particularly spent their money in drinking, going to the cinema, and buying clothing instead of buying their books for reading. A special and careful instruction in this regard is most important instead of simply offering jobs and money to the tribal people, otherwise the morality of the tribal people would be spoilt.

A careful examination shows that students who studied in the government institition have suffered a definite decline in the moral standards. The government schools lack in giving moral teachings and discipline as did the former mission schools. So the present system of government education does not seem to provide the right answer to meet the needs of young people in their moral education. A.S. Appasamy rightly says.

"With the tremendous expansion in education after Independence...the number of students have increased and the system has been watered down under the public examination system .... the system as it prevails today, therefore, has lost its religious, culture and philosophic moorings...the result has been the lowering of standard in the quality of education as a whole."[4]

The present young people of the Zeliangrongs are the product of government schools in which they were not fully fed

4. A.S. Appasamy : The Christian College in the llfe and awareness of the Church in India, (NCCR Vol. No. 13. October 1966), p. 405.

with mature education. Games and sports and compulsory working hours for all students which were given great importance in the former schools are being sadly neglected in most schools today. As a result, the suppressed energies of youth are directed to undesirable ends, resulting in lack of discipline, juvenile delinquency, the habit of drinking etc.

The so-called "cow-boy movies" where the world is presented to youth as a fighthing camp of conflicts and of adventures, have great influence on youth. The motive is to exploit the imagination of youth who love thrills and adventures. Today, we see many tribal boys dressed like cowboys, who love to act like cowboys. In some places gangs are formed resulting in fights. The Zeliangrong youth are not exempted from this fame.

The ideas of the Zeliangrong about God, Christ and Church are very vague and they have not been involved in and confonted by the Christian faith. The older Christians are usully conservative and reluctant to make changes. When any new ideas for youth programs are introduced, they view them with suspicion. Really the Church has responsibility to the lives of the youth to bring them to maturity in Christ in all areas of their lives.

We enter into a new year and into a new era of life. There is unrest and lack of discipline all over the country in the schools and colleges. We are living in a society of youth, a peculiar juncture of history where much that we once believed right is almost worng to them and much that we thought to be wrong is almost right to them. This is an age of new morality for young people. What are we doing for young people as a church ? It is a tragedy that we neither focus our attention on the problems of youth nor do any constructive thinking about them. We need to seriously concern ourselves with the youth people in the Church.

At present the pressure from the world around us is so strong that it forces our attention outside rather than within. It creates more complexities and confusion in society. Therefore, in such institutions, knowledge without purpose creates complicated problems. So let us rather pray for eye that see the vision, ears that hear the call and the hearts that obey.

Church in Relation to its Environment

We have said that the world is changing from the traditional way of living and belief to a liberal, modern, secular world which takes everything as natural. The Zeliangrong Church is in a transitional period. This is a confusing period. The old has not been completely demolished and the new has not yet fully taken shape. Everything is on the move. This period of change brings about crises in the life of the nation and the church as well. If one has no sense of balance and confidence, changes may lead to disaster. That is way there is a great need for a correct orientation in the life of the community and the Church.

The ratio of educated young men and women have been increasing rapidly. Now many students are in the High Schools, colleges and universities. Many have graduated. The potential of our self-hood as a nation is becoming evident. We can cite soms examples of the kinds of things that are happening not in self praise and conceit but by way of stating, perhaps, the possibility of further development of ourselves when we are given the opportunities. A few years ago, Mr. K. Gangmumei graduated in first position with an M.A. History from Gauhati University. Mr Liangsiyang made to the IAS; Mr. Dichamang Pamei, Mr. Khiamniyang Panmei have got MCS. Besides many others, men and women came to secure good Government High position as Doctors, Executive Engineers etc. Our people began to compete with the rest of the other advanced people in India. Our people are highly praised for getting the championship almost every year in the State Tournament in football and other games. Our young people began to participate in physical contests, dance competitions and other shows.

Under such a situation an untrained lay preacher becomes helpless and he is placed in an embarassing position before his people. He is unable to defend or refute. Therefore, we see a tremendous need for a well-trained and dynamic ministry for the Church. Well-trained and dedicated ministers, sensitive to the needs of the people, are urgently needed for leadership of the Zeliangrong Church today.

CHAPTER VI

Evaluation of Some Aspects of the Gospel in the Church

We are living in uncertain times, baffling and unpredictable. The Church is sepatated from involvement in a complex world. Therefore, our presentation of Christ must become integrally related to the struggle which is going on today. We will try to examine to what extent it is possible for the Church to renew her total life while she is part of the world.

Renewal of the Church for its Mission

What do we mean by renewal ? D.A. Thangasamy said, "Renewal is not merely the restoration of a life that has been waning, but an evalution and adaption of the environment and to make full creative use of the new opportunities have been gained"[1] It is in a deeper sense questioning and restating our response to God's demand. Under the renewal of the mission of our faith, it is the renewal of our corporate spiritual life, and involvement in the world.

The modern scientists have proclaimed that nature is not related to belief in the Christian conception of God's creation (Theory of evolution of Darwin). The rational knowledge and

1. D.A. Thangasamy : Renewal of the Cburch for its Mission; N.C.C,R. Vol. LXXXVII No. 4 (April 1967 page 135.

scientific outlook is surrounded by its own imperfect shadow of agnosticism, its doubts and hesitations about nature. On the other hand we have been fed by the Church for many decades. This has led to the strangest of attitudes against the secular world and against the achievement of science and theology. The realm of God and the realm of man have been divided and become irreconciliable, and implied that man stands permanently alienated from God.

In this situarion our approach and way of interpreting the message of God should be largely bassd in the way of our reconciling the achivement of science and secularity with our faith. Pro. Harvey Cox, in his book 'Secular City' pointed ouc that "the secular city, in which many problems are posed is part of God's great design."[2] So the Church should seek to understand that it relates its mission to it. We are compelled to regard God's cosmic plan for man's redemption as an integrated of whole which the secular world of science and technology are important elements. All of man's creative endeavour has to be viewed as part of a single pattern, not isolated, not over against but as element in it.

The Church is an the world and we are the Church, so the Church has to act as a leaven; it has to be the salt of the earth and illuminating centre in a distracted world. It is, therefore, the Church which should help the modern Christian hold his faith and the world in balance. Faith should be the response to trust and responsibility reposed in a man or a community. Even while Jesus was with his disciples. He invested them with responsibility for proclaiming the Gospel to the accompaniment of healing which called forth their faith in response. For the Church of today, faith then is a dynamic involvement in the affairs of the world in response to the trust God has placed in the Church for working with Him to redeem it.

2. Cox, Hurvey : The Secular City (Macmillan Company, New York) 1965.

The Zeliangrong Church needs to examine what is going on in this present age. The Church is not aware of the complexities of human behaviour. The Zeliangrong christians, as a whole, are straightforward and simple. They see what they see Truth for them is judged by sight and not by mind. Our faith in God must be renewed and awakened in relation to the new situation of this world.

Renewal of our Corporate Spiritual Life

The Church is composed of both individuals and the community of believers. It is not valued in terms of size or physical dimansion but in terms of its eternal mission and the inexaustible spiritual energy that it eminates to guide and inspire the life of any national group of which it is a part.

For a tribe like the Zeliangrong Nagas, life is unity : a solid social structure based on kinship system. This can be renewed and brought into the Fellowship within the body of Christ. The blood related families and villages, as a whole, can be a strong influence for a solid body of Christians among the Zeliangrongs. Since great importance is given to community in their lives, they contribute to the understanding of the Church as the community cooperate in the spirit of Christ.

Spirit and unseen power play a most prominent place in their belief. In fact they live a very spirit conscious life. This consciousness becomes so acute that it generates a fear complex as well. So the Church as the body of Christ must provide an atmosphere in which the Zeliangrong Christians can be conscious of the presence and power of the Holy Spirit of God. God, the unseen spirit, must be experienced within the conscious life of Christians. In other words, the body of Christ is and must be the framework within which the invisible but real powers of God become real to us.

The Zeliangrong socio-political organisation is an important factor. The Village Council, made up of all the head members of each clan, and the morung, the strongest youth organisation, are the major units. The election of officers at all organisations is carried out by religious rites. They village priest and the village headman are selected by the sprit himself. Once the person is selected to the office remains there and discharges his duty as faithfully as possible. The principle of unanimity is one of the most cherished practices in the body of Christ. So this might ease the group and personal tensions in their corporate spiritual life within the Church.

Involvement in the World

Our involvement in the world means renewal of our concern for national life. The 4th Assembly of the WCC of Upsala, Sweden (Italy 4-20, 1968) stressed the concern for the world. The theme of the Council was "behold, I make all things new". This theme was chosen in order to focus on the emerging situation of the crises and turmoils which demanded urgent action to stop and prevent actions against human dignity. Renewal of the Church, therefore, was seen in terms of what the world church should do to bolster up human values and integrate insights on the worship of God and the new style of living into programme of peace, justice and equality.

Keeping this fact in mind, the author is willing to consider some of the problems that arise between tribals and non-tribal cultures and their necessity of renewal in the life of the nation for the Christians.

The tribal peoples of India, as a whole, find their position in the nation to be quite different from the rest of the people. They live in constant fear and suspicion of the non-tribals. This attitude has been developed since the early times of the missionaries and the British officials. For this reason M.M. Thomas stated, "The difference with the non-tribals of India lies in the fact that whereas the non-tribals fait to respect the personality of the tribals, the western missionaries do respect the human personrlity and they also identify themselves with the tribals."[3] This may sound like an attempt to defend the position of Christian missionaries and the movement they presented in tribal areas but it is a fact which can hardly be denied, The late Prime Minister Nehru also referred in regard to the situation of the North-east India, he said, "The missionaries did a very good job there and I am full of praises for them, but politically speaking they did not particularly like changes in India."[4]

The lack of respect for the tribals as human persons in the past is more responsible than any other factors for the various reactions as manifested in political unrest in diflerent tribal areas in India today. It is a matter of common sense that when people become more educated and politically active even without any body's prompting they will be restive if they had been either exploited or humiliated in the past.

The tribals are, on the whole, simple and forthright by nature and temperament, and they are more pragmatic than philosophical. To them, as it should be to any right-minded person, actions speak louder than words. Therefore, to see that officers sent to the tribal areas are men and women of integrity, who can identify themselves with the tribal way of life, will be a satisfactory attempt.

On the part of the tribes like the Zeliangrongs, the need for realisation and responsibility toward their nation India as a whole is an immediate demand. Often in the papers we read statement such as, 'the minds of tribal people is in New York and London, not in New Delhi.' It seems to appear that their attitude and concern for their nation is not realised by them. The concern for the larger interest and the spirit of belonging together should not be lost sight of, and they should guard

3. M.M. Thomas & R.W. Layer : Tribal Awakening (Bangalore) 1965 pp. 202-3.
4. Nehru : Innaural address in Schedule Tribe & Schedule Areas Conference, New Delhi (June 1952) p. 17.

against the danger of being carried away too far by bitter and revengeful spirit. It is here that the Church which believes in the teaching of reconciliation should play a very important role. If the tribals are proud of their honesty, sincerity and integrity, they should not be afraid to mix with others, but rather serve as salt in the situation or light in the midst of darkness and transform she atmosphere of the present day.

The Zeliangrong and the tribal Church as a whole should be aware of the danger of being too loyal to its natural groupings and of the tendency towards 'tribalism'. The danger is in becoming too wrapped up in narrow tribal loyaties, thereby blurring true oneness in Chrirt with fellow-believers in India or in other countries. All are one because all the partners are in obedience to one Lord and one God whose one spirit energises and guides everyone.

Indigenisation

Zeliangrong Naga had no historical connection with Christ before Christianity was introduced to them. With the coming of Christianity their original way of life and culture died out. The reason for this is that the missionaries who came to the tribal areae regarded the tribal culture and traditions as associated with paganism and immoral practices. This belief caused them to abandon the rich culture of the Zeliangrong and adopted another so called "western Christian Culture". Furer-Haimendorf said in this context,

"Christianity and Nagas Culture seem to be oppsite poles, and on the side of the missionaries there have indeed been few attempts to bring the two into harmony and build on that which was valuable in tribal life. He furter said, but it may be that with a little more understanding and sympathy for Naga Culture they might have brought more happiness to their flock and avoided many of the more unfortunate results of a sudden clash of culture."[5]

5. C,V. Furer-Haimendorf : Nagas (Calcutta, 1913) p. 55.

In fact the white race was thought to be superior to the other races in the world. This superiority complex of the white man was made manifest even in the attitude, behaviour and dealings of the missionaries in relation to the tribals among whom they worked. The Western culture and ways have been completely adopted in the Churches, leaving aside their own indigenous culture and tradition.

Now the time has come to re-examine the position where the Church stands. It should not be forgotten that originality cannot be substituted by imitation. It should be borne in mind that Jesus Christ and His Gospel will never charge but the expression of its message should be relevant to the culture, thought and belief of the people. The possibilities for indigenisation in the Church can be discussed in the following :

1. *Song and Dance*

The outstanding feature in the Zeliangrong life is their love for singing and dancing. However these have been almost forgotten among the new generation of the Zeliangrong Christians. They have rich resources of music for worship and thanksgiving. There is devotional music which was to be sung by the priests only. There are many beautiful songs which can be adopted in the Church in worship. The spirit of their devotion and thanksgiving, music is to be brought to the service involving an indigenous setting for liturgy so that spiritual experience might be conveyed to their people in the art forms they understand best.

It seems, therefore, that some people who are well-versed in the Zeliangrong music and culture with the assistance some-one well-versed in western music, should devote time to making Zeliangrong Church Music. The Zeliangrong Christians should attempt to choose for themselves those types of aesthetic expressions which are more truly consonant with their new faith. The Zeliangrong Nagas express their joy and happiness in dance which can be used in giving thanks to God the almighty, the Creator as an expression of their deep gratitude and love to Him for His guidance and care.

2. *Faith*

The Zeliangrong Church has never taken serious thought to the formation of Christian teaching, faith and liturgy. Their pattern of thought and its liturgical setting have not yet been utilised and attempted in their worship in the Church. As a result some sorts of shallowness in understanding the true meaning of Christian faith in Christ are seen but should be built up in the way they understand best.

The Zeliangrong life was the celebration of nature's life cycle. All the year round as the vegetation and agriculture rotate, the religion and other aspects of life revolve around it. Physically they do live the seasonal rotation of life. And this has to be interpreted in the light of the inner existence.

C.V. Furer-Haimendorf writes, "I believe that even some of the old feasts and ceremonies—certainly the agricultural festivals could have been adopted by the Christian communities."[6]

Zeliangrong Nagas pray to the supreme deity known as 'Tingkauh Raguang' who is the Creator and good God who watches and guides the people, therefore, an appropriate Christian prayer might have been substituted and there seems to be no reason why at the beginning of the sowing of the crops and at the time when the harvesting is read the Zeliangrong Christian should not pray and give thanks to God for His bl essings.

Unless they have some basic inner relation between Christ and their culture the Zeliangrongs have no way to speak of them, however, it is the will of God for the Zeliangrongs that the worshipping community is the living culture which is the living witness of the presence of the incarnate Christ is the

6. Op. cite. p. 57.

Zeliangrong Culture. It is the new creation among us, and this community is the hope, faith and love in Christ.

3. *Architecture*

It may be noted, as a sing of the ti nes, the beginning of an attempt to use the Zeliangrong style of architecture in building their Church is undertaken. The present building style which is maintained comes from Europe and though no doubt good and impressive, to keep in touch with the more familiar, with heir indigenous ideas and thoughts in worship, the Zeliangrong style of building will serve the purpose. Their style of building is very attractive. The front side of the house is raised up high enough and lowered down at the closed end, and the roof almost touches the around which looks like the sitting position of a dog. The carving of wood and figures decorated on the front wall might be diverted to Christian arts. It seems to be of no reason why the Zeliangrong Church should not build their Church in such a way that they can see their own traditional way of wood carving just as medievel craftsmen decorated Gothic Cathedrals with fabulous animals, gargoyles and domons so that the expert wood carvers and builders among the Zeliangrongs can use the traditional style with advantage in building their house of worship. And the worshippers will feel more quite at home and eassily express their faith and devotion to their God Almighty.

Dr. Hutton also suggested for the Baptist Churches of Nagas that colour and brilliant effects which the Nagas possess can be turned to the glory of God instead of being regarded as an offence before Him. If the bright clothes, worn as a reward for the giving of feasts of merit by the ancient, were retained by the Cristians for their acts of social services; if the insignia of renown in war were made badges of rank in the congregation, and deacons and pastors encouraged to wear horn-bill feathers, cowries and aprons to denote their office while those assembling for dining worship were encouraged to do honour to the occassion in their best, if they were encouraged to adorn their

Church building with carvings as they have done their morungs and their long dorms in the past, it is hard for a layman to see how the deity would be dishonoured thereby while their unqestionable artistic sense would be encouraged and possibly imbued with fresh vigour.

It is high time for the Zeliangrnng Church to look back and rethink as to how well their Church should be managed in the way their people think and the belief in which they have been brought up without breaking the heart of the Gospel. Christ wants the inner heart, the originality out of which flows the message to quench the thirsty heart.

Zeliangrong Church in the Future

When one pauses to think of the Zeliangrong Church present and future, one recognises afresh the great magnitude of God's love and grace. The Zeliangrong were a people who walked in darkness but now have seen a great light. They have nothing to be afraid of whatever insurmountable difficulties may come in their ways if they have firm and unshakeable faith in the steadfast love of God. They are uncertain but their future belongs to God in whom they trust.

The Zeliangrong Naga Christians need to ponder seriously the following suggestions if they went to communicate the Gospel of Christ effectively to the people.

1. There is a multiplicity of diversity in increasing knowledge and division, There is political unrest and crises in the area. They should seiously think and judge as true Christians and work towards closer cooperation and unity.

2. Encourage the most promising and brilliant young people to attend colleges and seminaries and enter full-time ministry. Scholarships should be provided and future prospects made alluring to them.

3. Create a genuine interest in social concern; bodly speak for righteousness and fearlessly condemn evil.

4. Rapid indigenistion of the Zeliangrong Church is very important. There is need for making Christianity intelligible and relevant to the people in terms of the only life they know. There should be strong emphasis on Christian stewardship of time, talent and money which is the source of self-support and self-propagation.

5. The Zeliangrong Church needs a sound and strong ministry. Most of the people have very hazy ideas of God, Jesus Christ, Church and the Bible. They should be properly educated in the knowledge of the faith.

6. As Christians they should come out of their narrow 'tribal ghettos' and seek wider unity with fellow Christians in India and around the world.

7. Finally the author would like to emphasise the great need for strong Christian institutions. This should aim to produce good Christian laymen for the next generation, who will become the pillars of their Church and leaders of the country tomorrow. Money and efforts can best be invested in establishing good Christian schools. Realising this some of the devoted Christian groups and Churches have established Christian schools. This seems to be the most urgent need of the hour.

The task before the Zeliangrong people is colossal. But they are not to be afraid for they are not alone. Their confidence stems from the assurance given by the Lord when He said, "Lo, I am with you always, till the end of the age."

CHAPTER VII

Biographies Namrijinang Kamei Maipak

K. Namrijinang alias Maipak was born in 1874 in the village of Khokiu in Tamenglong District, Manipur. This village is no more in existence. His father's name was Dikhonang Kamei and mother's name was Poumengliu. His mother died when Namrijinang was a small boy. He was thus brought up by father. A deadly disease spread out in the Khokiu village. In order to escape from sickness his father shifted to Aling Nam. From there he migrated to Khudeipon at Imphal Valley. As Dikhonang Kamei was so much concerned for his only son he tried to get a job for him in the Palace of the Manipur Maharaja Ningthem (Sir Churand/KCSI) and put him there under the care of the Maharaja. Before long, his father died leaving Namrijinang an orphan.

Namrijinang worked as a carpenter along with an other service in the Maharaja's Palace. In 1902 he joined the Maharaja's band party as a bugler. Because of his efficiency and skill in his given task he was given promotion as major in the Bugler Band. He worked under the Maharaja in this position upto 1912.

There was a man, Hiraji, and his daughter Pantigongliu. They were also living in the Palace working under the Maharaja.

Namrijinang married Pantigongliu. Sons and daughters were born to them, three to four times, but none of them lived. All died in infancy. As a result there was no peace of mind in the family. He consulted many priests both Meiteis and Tribals to help their problems, but no success. He asked his wife and consulted that they should seek the true God who would bless them give issues to his wife. While he was seeking the true religion and God, the Lord made a way for them. There was a Christian named Bhagirath Gurya from Sudya, Assam; who came as a teacher for the Maharaja Band Party. He taught about Jesus Christ and asked Namrijinang to become a Christian. A Bengali gospel tract was given him to read. During this time William Pettigrew, the first Missionary was already in Imphal. He went to the Missionary and enquired about Chrlst and its religion. Namrijinang Maipak believed and accepted Jesus Christ as his personal Saviour in 1914. In this same year in December a son was born to them who was named Kaphunlung David which means the living seed.

On December 6, 1915, Namrijinang Maipak was given water Baptism by U.M. Fox. He declared, "It is amazing to my soul—I was in bondage of darkness and sin, but now, in the love sacrifice of my Lord Jesus on the cross of Calvery, I have been given the light of Heaven and eternal life." On January 19, 1916, his wife Pantiguangliu was also given baptism by William Pettigrew. Thus the whole family got wonderful experience of happiness and peace as they accepted new lives in Christ Jesus.

Namrijinang was still employed by the Maharaja and the family settled at Keisamthong Rongmei village, Imphal. The first Church in Manipur was thus planted in Keisamthong village in 1916. They built a small thatch Church in the village where 18 Christians came to worship regularly. Every sunday the bell chimed to call the people to worship. From time to time William Pettigrew came to preach to them and worshipped together with the believers.

Because of his new faith in Jesus Christ, the villagers of Keisamthong strongly opposed him and in every possible way they tried to pressurise him to renounce his faith in Jesus Christ. He was insulted and they cursed the name of Jesus. They began to force him to obey and showed all "Genna" and strict order was given not to practise worship and singing in the Church. He was forced to pay many subscriptions to the village during festivals and worship of the village gods; If he were not to oblige he would be driven away from the village. Namrijinang Maipak bore patiently all those impositions. But charging that he did not obey the orders of the village, the boys of the village Morung aroused against him and all his family properties, clothing, utensils were thrown out of the Village by force. However he was not seriously tortured or man-handled. The Lord had been always with him and saved him from torture to death. At the same time Namrijinang was loved and taken care of by the Manipur Maharaja. He was in this village for three more years after his conversion enduring much suffering and shame in the hand of the Keisamthing villagers.

Namrijinang Maipak knowing he would not be allowed to live in the village permanently, went to approach Sir Churachand Maharaja (KCSI) to give some land were his band of Christian can settle and live. The Maharaja was kind to him. He was allotted a land measuring 7½ acres for all the Christians to settle at Thangmeiband. Thus the Christian group came and settled there and they also constructed a Church building. This Church was dedicated on April 20, 1917 and began to be known as Thangmeiband Christian colony. This was the second Church building constructed in the Imphal valley. They also established a primary school, hostel and guest house for the Christians. The first pastor of the Thangmeiband Church was Prom Singh. The first teacher of the School was Kaboklei (Mrs.) and the first evangelist was Namrijinang Maipak. Those Christians who settled at Thangmeiband Christian colony were meitei, Rongmei, Tangkhul, Kom and Gorkha. They were all together seven families in numbers. They were all from different tribal groups and speaking different dialects but in the name of Jesus Christ, they all lived together in love and in one accord. When Namrijinang was in the Thangmeiband Christian colony, his wife gave birth again to a son on September 2, 1917. They named him Kachinggongpou Peter.

As Namrijinang was still working for the Maharaja, during the first great world war of 1914-1918, he went for war to France as 'The Manipur Labour Corp', on May 15, 1917. By the time he returned from war, as a credential for his good and faithful service, the British Government awarded to Namrijinang Maipak four Medals.

In 1918 Namrijinang Maipak, as a good soldier of Christ, together with Tongul brought and preached the Gospel of Jesus Christ to the Government Outpost of Oinamlong at Tamenglong District. In the Outpost a man named Jinlakpou from Kaikao village was employed as care-taker. He heard the Gospel and believed it and became Christian. This was the first fruit of Namrijinang's labour among the Zeliangrong Nagas.

Namrijinang Maipak gave up active service from Sepoy on May 15, 1919 and entered into the full time evangelistic work of the Gospel of Christ. In same year on December 5, his third son born whose name was Kaninglung Stephen. As employed by the missionaries, Namrijinang Maipak as an evangelist began to tour village to village in the Zeliangrong area in Tamenglong District, preaching the love Gospel of Christ to his own people.

In 1919 when the military Outpost was set-up to protect Kuki rebellion in Tamenglong areas the Civil Sub-divisional Officer (Britisher) and its head-quarter was established. When the civil peace and tranquility was re-established in the Zeliangrong areas, Mr. Namrijinang Maipak went from village to village throughout the area bringing the first good news of the

Gospel of Christ to his own people whom he contacted. Very Soon, a young man, Zinlakpou, from Kaikao village, who was employed by the Government in the S.D.O. office heard the Gospel eariier from the Out-post Oinamlong came forward to accept the Lord Jesus as his personal Saviour and got baptised in 1920. He was the first fruit of convert among the Zeliangrongs in Manipur. Now he in turn went to his village and proclaimed the name of Jesus as the Saviour of the world and human kind. Thus withhout much delay ten families became Christians and within two year the family members doubled to twenty. Now the strong opposition from the villagers came and drove away the Christians from the village. The S.D.O. of Tamenglong ordered the Christians to leave the village within the week with a fine of Rs 400/-. William Pettigrew requested the Christians to shift to a safe place and establish a Christians village known as Sempang. This was the first Christian Church planted in the Zeliangrong land in Manipur. Namrijinang Maipak was sent to this village by William Pettigrew to work as teacher-evangelist among the Zeliangrongs. The Sempang Church was organised to be a full-fledged Church on September 26, 1924. A way was established and opened that Mr. Pakho Sitlou and Mr. Plan were called to be the teachers in the School at Sempang Baptist, Church.

Namrijinang's wife gave birth again to a girl on August 13, 1922 who was named Nurjahan Mary. However, the Lord had taken her back home soon on July 21, 1924. She was the first baby among the Zeliangrong in Manipur who died as a Christian and buried in name of Jesus Christ. In the same year the family of Namrijinang shifted to Tamenglong head-quarter where he worked as carpenter in the Bungalow of S.D.O. office. He also, with other friends, engaged in the construction of the S.D.O. Office and repairing. In that way he earned money by himself and from time to time, he went out to the villages for preaching the Gospel. He also witnessed about Jesus to whoever came to work with him. Many times he went to the

Morungs of the Tamenglong Village where with a picture roll of Jesus Christ witnessed and preached to the young people. The villagers raised against him thinking that he had brought the picture of demons. He was charged as a bed men and not to stay in the village. Thus he was driven out of the Village. He went away from the village and climbing to a small hill sang songs with thanksgiving and prayed to the Lord for the villagers, who were spiritually blind, to forgive their sins.

The hymn he sang was 'Blessed assurance" S.S. 873. His singing was strange and beautiful. The young men by name Mr. Hurong and Mr. Laibam heard his singing and listened to him carefully. This was the first Gospel which was shown to the Tamenglong Village, the biggest village in the Zeliangrong area. In short, in 1929 Mr. Hurong and his friends accepted Jesus Christ during Christmas time at Sempang Baptist Church. In 1930 worship Place for the Tamenglong village was established on the hill where Namrijinang sang and prayed for the villagers. Thus the blessing of God from above to His people poured down on Tamenglong Village.

Namrijinang Maipak got another son on Oct 15, 1927, which was the fourth son to them. Again on September 9, 1930 a daughter was born. The name of the children were Nigthoi and Nganditon respectively. However his daughter Nganditon expired and was taken back home to Heaven on March 7, 1931.

Namrijinang Maipak went to preach not only among his own Zeliangrong people but also among other tribals. He went to the South of Manipur among the Anal Nagas. In 1925 he preached in the village called Mitang where for the first time in the history of South-east of Manipur Mr. Kowak Ngaren and L. Thomchung received the Gospel. As his second ministry, he went with one of his evanglists from Thangmeiband Christian Colony to Tamenglong Head-Quarters along with his family. He continued to preach and witness Jesus in many villages in

Zeliangrang areas. When the Japanese war (2nd world war) broke out he and his family went to Taothingjang on the bank of the Barak rivers and settled there for some years but it was too hot for them at the same time for a few families living in the remote jungle was impossible so they came back to Tamenglong village. It was in 1944, on June 9, at about midnight he gave up his soul to Christ at 70 years old. His burial service was performed by the Tamenglong Village Baptist Church. After a fruitful labour for Christ he had completed the course and went to rest in Heaven where his master Jesus prepared for him. His wife Pantigongliu also died in December 1952 at the age of 78. The funeral service was performed by the Kgongjaron Baptist Church and she was buried at the same village.

Pakho Sitlou

Pakho Sitlou was an outstanding evangelist and Christian leader among the Thadous. He was one of the pioneer missionaries of the Thadou Kukis, who was sent as a missionary to the non-Thadou communities. He was sent as first evangelist by the American Baptist Mission to preach the Gospel among the Kabui Nagas (Ronomeis) and to help the early Rongmei believers of the Kaikao village. Pakho accepted the Lord Jesus Christ as his personal saviour at his maternal uncle's village, Tongkoi. He was baptised by William Pettigrew on Dec. 12, 1913 while he was studying at Ukhrul M.E. School.

Pakho Sitlou, like any other youth, had great plans and ambitions relative to the success he would be in the profession of his choice. He dreamt of climbing the educational ladder until he became a government officer. However God wanted him to preach. Since his early schooldays, there was the call of God upon him. There was a moving of God's spirit upon him and God showed him the worth of a soul and the enternal dividends to be received by one who gives himself whole-heartedly to the Lord's business. As the power of God was upon him he felt the cry in his own heart, Lord "Here am I, send me." Then he had surrendered to preach the Gospel or do anything; go anywhere, to enter the full-time work of an evangelist. He first started to work among the people of Sadar Hills. He was then sent as first evangelist by Dr. G.G. Crozier to work among the Kabui Nagas (Rongmeis). On March 31, 1924, he reached Kaikao, a Zeliangrong Naga Village.

The early Rongmei Christians of Kaikao village had founded a village called Sempang. Pakho planted the organised Church at Sempang and set up an upper primary school there. Sempang became the most important educational and religious centre. Here, many people young and old came to take liberal education and learn the words of God and Gospel music.

In appreciation of his service, the Rongmeis of Sempang offered Pakho one of their dearest daughters. He received favour from the Lord and found a godly wife. Pakho had mastered Rongmei language. Pakho is the architect of the Rongmei literature. He compiled the Gospel song book 'Raguang Lu' (God's song). He rendered some of the Thadou spirituals and the four gospels into Rangmei dialect.

In the early period of his Gospel campaign, the political situation in all the hill areas of Manipur was quite distressing. The relation between the Nagas and the Thadous was severed as mutual distrust and jealousy arose out of the political manœuvre of the Britishers who, exploiting the abnomal situation, intended to suppress the turbulent hill tribes and bring them under their way. The political and social condition which was far from normals had been aggravated by the British government that enacted ordinance that massive force labour corps should be formed and sent to France to supplement their fighting capacity during the First world war. The Thadou Kukis unwilling to go abroad and refusing the enactment of the Ordinance, revolted against the British Government with strong hands. Howevert the situation was still in turmoil and chaos. The inter-village feuds and disputes were not uncommon.

Murder, arson and burglary were rampant and life was extremely insecure. Mutual suspicion and fears were still predominant.

During this period of crisis, Pakho began preaching the words of God among the Heathens of North-western part of Manipur. The western part of Manipur, the North-west Tamenglong sub-division were populated by several communities such as the Rongmeis, Liangmeis, Thadous, Chirus Koms and Marams. As people of different communities came to accept Jesus as their personal saviours, the social distinctions, cultural differences and racial prejudices had broken down. A new society based on the excellency of the knowledge of Christ was established. Pakho went on preaching the Gospel with the untiring real from village to village and organising Churches. The children of God multiplied and many churches grew, which culminated in the formation of the West Christian Association, consisting of all the Christians of different communities — Thadous, Rongmeis and Liangmei Nagas, Hmars, and Chirus. He worked as Superintendent Pastor from 1930.

After working for more than fifteen years in the south of North-west, Tamenglong sub-division, on July 21, 1939 he left Sempang and worked among the Liangmei Nagas and Thadous of North-west of Manipur with Lamlaba as a base. After rendering fervent and selfless service among the Zeliangrong Nagas for twenty-five years he left Lamlaba and returned to his village Taloulong (Kaipu) in 1947. Under his wise and inspiring leadership Talouloog Church emerged into a full-fledged organised Church, having eleven churches during his life time.

With the increase of Christian population, the North-west Christian Association field became very vast. It required proper evaluation to solve verious problems of the growing Christian population with different social backgrounds. Moreover, the need for effective evangelism through different dialects was keenly felt. For the sake of convenient administration and effective witness in 1947 the North-west Christian Association came to be divided into two viz. Kuki Christian Association and Zeliangrong Baptist Association. Since then Pakho worked in the capacity of Superintendent Pastor among his own people till he retired from active service in 1957 due to his deplorable health.

He wished to do service to his Master till his last breath. Even illness and old age could not keep him down. On April 29, 1962, this man of God went into the presence of the King whom he had so faithfully served to receive his reward. Pakho was truly poor in his earthly goods and comforts yet he made many rich. For him soul-winning is the all consuming desire of his heart.

Maisi Newmei

Mr. Maisi, son of Hulungbou, was born at Hiujiulong (Ningzam) Village in July 1895. His father died while he was very young. So he was brought up by his grandfather. He came to know the Lord Jesus Christ through the witness of a Hmar Christian and he accepted Jesus as his personal Saviour in 1925. This record was found in the hand of Darlal, pastor of Zoute, a Hmar village. He went to Kangpokpi Christian Mission Shcool for studies in the same year. After four yeras of his studies in the School, he was sent back by Dr. G.G. Crozier, the then American Baptist Missionary, to evanglise among his people in his village.

Maisi also went along with Dr. Crozier in all the Zeliangrong areas in witnessing and preaching the Gospel of Christ. This was the first occassion for the white American Missionary to set foot in the Zeliangrong soil. Dr. Crozier, as a missionary, helped many sick people in the village where medical facility absolutely nil in those days. Mr. Maisi continued to work as an evangelist for three years among the Liangmeis in the northern parts of the Zeliangrong Area.

In 1932-33, the whole Zeliangrong areas was alighted by the movement of Haipou Zadonang and Rani Gaidinliu which effected the Zeliangrong areas seriously that the preaching of the Gospel was very much hampered. Maisi went down to Sempang Village in 1932 and worked as teacher-preacher and in 1933 at Sangrungpang Village. He also took a wife from the Sangrungpang Village.

Mr. Maisi was appointed a Government school teacher by the British Government. He was the first teacher among the Zeliangrong Nagas. He was posted at Lamlaba and worked as a teacher in the governmeut Primary School since 1933 up till 1938. Though he was a Government employee he never forgot to witness Jesus where-ever he stayed and where-ever he worked. He was then transferred to Tamenglong Head-quarter and continued to teach in the Government Middle English School till he retired from activs service in 1967. He actively worked as a church deacon and pastor in the Town Baptist Church, Tamenglong since 1940-1970 (1940-41. deacon; 1942-44 pastor; 1945-54, deacon; 1955-70, pastor).

Mr. Maisi was a very meek and humble leader. His affection and love for his people was very much appreciated by the whole Zeliangrong Nagas. He was a peace-loving person and he had never quarrelled with anyone. He also mastered all the different dialects of the Zeliangrong Nagas. Thereby, he could communicate the Gospel effectively everywhere he went. His personal age is 95 years now. He is still strong and active. He life was a blessing to his Zeliangrong brothers and sisters.

A. Pariwangbou

Mr. A. Pariwangbou alias Matikbo was born in 1902 at Longdi Papram village. Through the preaching of a Kuki Christian, he became a Christian in 1924. He was a genuine Christian actively devoting his life to Jesus Christ and witnessing him faithfully in his capacity in his local village. Knowing that Pariwangbou was committed to the service of the Gospel he was appointed to as head evangelist by the North-west Baptist Association (Zeliangrong) in 1929 and he continued to preach about Jesus in the Zeliangrong field upto 1957. He was a committed and honest servant of God in the Zeliangrong field.

Mr. Pariwangbou was also the first convert of the Longdi Papram village and also the first Christian among the Liangmei Naga in Manipur. He served as Chairman of the Liangmei Naga Christian Literature Society for Manipur and Nagaland,

He took his last breath on 21st May, 1981 and took rest in the Lord when he was 80 years old.

Bibliography

Albaugh Dana M. : *Between the Century* : The Judson Press, Chicago, 1935.

Alemchiba M. : *A brief Historical Account of Nagaland* : Naga Institute of Culture, Kohima, Nagaland.

Boston William Cammell : *History of American Baptist Mission* : Gould, Kendall and Lencoln 59 Washington Street 1849.

Bower U.G. : *Drums Behind the Hills* : William Morrow and Comp. New York, 1950.

Bower, U.G. : *Naga Path* : John Murry 50 Albemarie at London 1950.

Brown, R. : *Staistical Account of Manipur Valley* : London 1874 (Reprint 1976 Delhi).

Chakravorty, B.C. : *British Relation with the Hill Tribes of Assam since 1858*, Firma K.L. Mukhopadhay, Calcutta 1964.

Clerk, Mar Mead : *A Corner in India* : Philadelphia American Publication Society, 1907.

Dusanu : *Naga for Christ* : Assam Printing Works Private Limited 1989.

Dalton, E.T. : *Descriptive Ethnology of Bengal* : Calcutta 1872.

Dozo, Phuveyi : *Hill Tribes now for Tribes in India* : NMM, Nagaland Baptist Church Council, 1989.

Down, Fredrick : *The Mighty Works of God* : Christian Literature Centre. Pan Bazar, Gauhati.

Downs, Fredrick : *Christianity in North-East India* : ISPIC, New Delhi 1983.

Elwin, V. *The Nagas in the Nineteenth Century* : Oxford University Press, 1969.

Elwin, V. The Tribal World of Verrier Elwin : Oxfyrd University Press, 1964.

Evans, G.L. and James *Imphal* : London Macmillan & Co. Ltd. 1962.

Furer-Haimendorf, C.V. *Naked Nagas* : Thacker, Sink & Co. Ltd. 1962.

Gangumei Kabui *Jadonang* : 1990.

Ghosh, B.B. *History of Nagaland* : S. Chand & Co. Ltd. 1982.

Harvey Cox *Secular City* : Macmillan & Co, New York, 1965.

Hodson, T.C. : *Naga Tribes of Manipur* : London, 1911.

Johnson J. : *My Experience in Manipur and Naga Hills* : London, William Clows & Sons 1896.

Kadi Mpamei A. : *Hermon Chingkhou Zikdiu* : Dimaond Jubilee Publication, Tamenglong 1989.

T. Luikham : *A Short History of the Manipur Baptist Christian Golden Jubilee* : North-east Christian Association, Ukhrul, Manipur 1948.

McCuloch Col. : *Account of the Valley of Monipur*: London 1858.

Namthiurei M.P. : *The Great Awakening* : Jubilee Publication, Christian Centre, Khongjaron, Tamenglong 1970.

Nehru : *Inaugural Address in the Schedule Tribe and Schedule caste Areas Conference* : New Delhi 1952.

Philip T.R. : *The growth of Baptist Church in Nagaland.*

Prim Suantak Vaiphei : *Church growth among the Hill Tribes* : Goodwill Press, Imphal 1979.

Reid, R. : *History of the Frontier Areas Bordering on Assam from 1883-1941*, Shillong 1942.

Ringkaho Lolly R. *The Baptist Church in Manipur* : Modern Printer, Imphal, 1985.

Smith O.J. : *The Passion for Soul* : Marshall, Morgan & Scott.

Roy, J. : *History of Manipur* : Firma K.L. Mukhapadhay Calcutta 1958.

Shimray, R.R. : *Origin and Culture of Nagas* : Samsik Publications, New Delhi 1989.

Thomas, M.M. & Taylor : *Tribal Awakening* : CISRS, Bangalore 1965.

Visor, H. : *The Naga Baptist Family* : Council of Naga Baptist Churches, Kohima, Nagaland 1988.

J. V, Hluna : *Church and Political Upheaval in Mizoram* : Mizo History Association, Aizawl 1985.

Benrew : Baptist Church Diamond Jubilee Reha, 1981, Labanya Art Press, Dimapur.

Thesis

Andeson Bengt Ivar : *American Missions Evangelisation of the Nagas* : Northern Baptist Theo. Seminary 1965.

Imchaba Bendang Wati : *Christian among the Nagas* : Northern Baptist Theological Seminary 1948.

Namthomang Kamei : *A brief note on Zeliangrong Nagas' Tradition and Culture* : Tamenglong 1962.

Namthiurei Daimei : *The Ethno History of Zeliangrong Nagas*: A dissertation submitted to M.U. toward the degree of M. Phil 1989.

Gonmei, Peace : *The Culture and Religious life of Rongmei Nagas & Christianity*: E.T.C. Jorhat 1989.

Shishak, Tuishem Awungchi : *Development of Christian Leaders among Naga Tribes* : Northerh Baptist Theological Seminary 1961.

A separate Zeliangrong Administrative Unit, Memorandum submitted to the Prime Minister of India Tamenglong, Manipur 1964.

Memorandum submitted to Hon'ble Prime Minister of India Shri Rajiv Gandhi, Zeliangrong People's Convention ι Rani Gaidinliu, New Delhi, 1986.

Memorandum submitted to Shri S.C. Jamir, Chief Minister of Nagaland, Kohima, 1989.

Reports

Assam Mission (American Baptist Missionary Union) Paper and Discussion of the Conference, Nowgong 1886.

Reports of the Council of Baptist Churches in Assam and Manipur, 1955 , 1956, 1957, 1958, 1959 : These are published by the Secretary of CBCAM, Gauhati.

Reports of the Council of Baptist Churches in North East India.

Reports of the Council of Baptist Churches In North East India 1960, 1961, 1962, 1964, 1965, 1968. These are published by the Secretary of the CBCNEI, Gauhati.

Report of North Eastern Frontier of British India (Reprint 1966, Gauhati).

Periodicals

National Christian Council Review, Monthly Magazine, Oct. 1966, April 1967.

The first Zeliangrong Catholics Students' Conference 1989, Tamenglong District, Manipur.

Resolution

North-west Christian Assciation meeting Resolution 1, 1933-1954, Tamenglong.

Minute

North-west Baptist Christian Assn. Pator's Conference, Churches and other meetings minutes, Miscellaneous, Book I Tamenglong.

Index

A. Z. Keneise, 54
Anderson, B. L., 101
Assam, Zeliangrong Nagas, 60-61
Baptist Church, the establishment of, 48-49
Beers, R. G., 99
Bible Society of India, 105-106
Bible school, 97-98
British rule, the establishment of, 43-44
Brock, Earl E., 90-91
Christians, the persecution of, 49-50
Chiroistian, Missionaries, educational work, 83-84
Christian association, division of circles, 100-101
Christian centre, the establishment of, 92-93
Christian Missionaries, later development, 90-91
Christian teachings, adoption of, 115-116
Christian youth, effect of education, 117-118
Christianity, the first convert, 45-46
Church Auxiliary for Social Action, 84-85
Church, impact of modern secular trends, 116-117
Church, its environment, 120-121
Church, organisation of, 88-89
Church, renewal of mission, 122-123
Corporate spritual life, 124-125
Council of Baptist Churches in North-East India, 93-94
Dinthuiyang, 88
Eliangrong union, 109-110
Finny, Chas c., 76
Gangmumei, K, 120-121
Gospel, the first communication, 42, 82
Hills, N. C. 80
Indian Church, the current problem, 101-102
Jorhat Bible School, 106-107
KANGPOKPI Mission Centre, 81-82
Kadi, Mpamei, 62
Kukis rebellion, 47-48
Laokeinang, 88

Liangmei Naga, 97
Liangmel Baptist Association, 56- 57
Malunmei, 30-31
Malunmei, two kinds, 31-32
Manipur Baptist Association, 93-94
Manipur, background history, 14-15
Matikbou, 88
Missionaries, leadership training, 86-87
Missionaries, second World War, 87
Mission work, reinforcement of, 63
Missionaries, the arrival of, 43-44
Missonaries, the early work, 66-67
Morung, 30
Naga tribes, .971 census
Nagaland and Assam, begining of Chiristianity, 53-54
Nagaland, background history, 9-10
Nagaland, origin as state, 11-12
Nagaland, the British takeover, 12
Nagaland, the creation, 11
Nagaland, the revival movement, 62-63
Nagas, the Tenyime group, 13- 14
Nagas, the migration of, 13-14
Nagas, tribes and clans, 11-12
Namdailong Baptist Church, 74-75
Namrijinang, K. 133-141
Namrijinpou, Kamei, the first convert, 45-46
Newmei, Maisi, 142-143
Nurjahan Mary, 137
Pamei, Bikau, 64-65
Pariwangbou, A., 143-144
Pettigrew, William, 81
Puimei, 97
Revival movement, socio-economic awareness, 79-80
Revival movement, the effects, 74-75
Revival movement, the outcome, 72-73
Rongmei Naga, 97
Rongmei Baptist Association, 58-59
Rose, J. A., 106-107
Sahu, Subodh, 70-71
Shaw, R. H., 51
Shing, N. K,, 107
Silcher Valley, Rongmei, 65-66
Simon, K. G., 107
Simon, K. G. 98
Sitlou, Pakho, 139-140
Smith, Oswald J. 81-82
Tekhao, 88
Visor. A, 53
Welsh Presbyterin Missionaries, 61-62
Women's society, Zeliangrong, 99-100
Zeliangrong, the land, 16-17
Zeliangrong, Annual Association meeting, 89-90
Zeliangrong Baptist Association, 53.

Zeliangrong Baptist Churches Council, 94-95
Zeliangrong Nagas, characteristics, 113-114
Zeliangrong Nagas, social life, 28-29
Zeliangrong Nagas, the literature, 103-104
Zeliangrong People's Convention, 11
Zeliangrong Church, future, 131-132
Zeliangrong rebellion, 36
Zeliangrong, architecture, 130-131
Zeliangrong, demand for homeland, 110-1I1
Zeliangrong. economic development, 111-112
Zeliangrong, economic life, 26-27
Zeliangrong, ethinicity, 4-5
Zeliangrong, faith, 129-130
Zeliangrong, formation of union, 108-109
Zeliangrong, howering past, 6-7
Zeliangrong, indigenisation, 127-128
Zeliangrong, life after death, 35-36
Zeliangrong, life of people, 18-19
Zeliangrong, linguistic attributes, 4-7
Zeliangrong, music and dance, 25-26
Zeliangrong, orign of the people, 17-18
Zeliangrong, religious ideas, 34-35
Zeliangrong, social landscape, 4-8
Zeliangrongs, history, 1-9
Zemei Naga, 97

9788185565682